D1355899

HAWKINGE
1912–1961

An in depth history of the former Royal Air
Force Station Hawkinge

ROY S. HUMPHREYS

MERESBOROUGH BOOKS
1981

Published by Meresborough Books, 7 Station Road, Rainham, Gillingham, Kent. ME8 7RS. Medway (0634) 371591.

Meresborough Books specialize in the publication of books on Kent local history. Fifteen books are currently in print with more scheduled for publication Summer and Autumn 1981. In addition Meresborough Books publish a monthly journal on all aspects of Kent local history "Bygone Kent". Full details from your local bookshop or direct from Meresborough Books.

KENT AIRFIELDS IN THE BATTLE OF BRITAIN

By The Kent Aviation Historical Society

Published as a uniform edition with this book, also at £5·95. Available from your local bookshop or direct from Meresborough Books at £6·40 post free.

Printed and bound by Mackays of Chatham Ltd.

CONTENTS

INTRODUCTION

In the eighteenth century the village of Hawkinge, as we know it today, was known as Uphill, a small hamlet with its windmills and mill green surrounded by trees that stretched away in all directions as far as the eye could see. It was a quiet almost insignificant hamlet situated on top of the North Downs some four miles from the English Channel, with dusty cart tracks crossing at its centre, a little known parish that few people visited.

The nineteenth century brought little change to the area. The most notable event which took place in October each year was the Statute Fair held on the village green. At this fair servants were hired to the wealthy land owners, particularly to the owners of Flegges Court, a large Manor house of some importance situated to the East in the original village. This had changed its name from Haverkyng to Hackinge and then finally to Hawkinge.

At the turn of the century aviation, then in its infancy, took a foothold on pasture land to the West of Uphill. It was a flat expanse of rich grass divided into eleven small fields and bordered by the familiar hedges and trees which epitomised the small farm holdings in our agricultural areas.

Sir Charles Igglesden, writing in the early twenties, described Hawkinge as the Headquarters of air defence against German attack during the Great War period. He also went on to suggest that the large hangars were erected secretly, protected and guarded from the German spy. Both statements were far from the truth. In the first instance the aerodrome never held a home defence squadron and, secondly, can you imagine building six enormous hangars and other administrative buildings in such a rural setting without anyone's knowledge!

Ironically the first aviator to set foot in the village was a foreigner, a Dutchman called Megone, who arrived four years before the Great War started. Rejecting any sort of publicity he chose to work in comparative secrecy and seclusion, inventing flying machines which could be used for military application. This was the period in aviation history when competitions and prizes were being offered for the best designs, the Government having issued certain specifications for such a machine. Strange as it may seem the Dutchman entered none of these and his subsequent and somewhat silent disappearance just before the outbreak of World War I was, to say the least of it, a trifle baffling.

Many years have passed since the arrival of Megone, to be followed by the Royal Flying Corps and the Royal Air Force, and, as one reflects over those years, one feels a pang of sadness that the aerodrome no longer exists. There are those who remember with deep gratitude the unselfishness, the courage and sheer guts of the men who flew from and worked at the aerodrome. During the inter-war years they, and certainly those who came after them, constantly and triumphantly displayed their mastery of technique to the rest of the world.

It is a mammoth task to record within these pages all the exploits of these men and their squadrons or units but, suffice it to say, I have covered almost every kind of duty which was performed at RAF Hawkinge, both in peace and war. These duties range from the normal training programme of peace-time squadrons and on to the more skilled aerobatics and air displays. Then, with the outbreak of the Second World War, came the fighter patrols of the Battle of Britain period; the reconnaisance patrols carried out by the famous 'Jim Crow' squadron; the air sea rescue patrols; the anti-submarine and convoy protection patrols; the V1 interceptions and bomber escort duties.

All of these duties were carried out from RAF Hawkinge and, as a front-line station throughout the last war, it saw action unfold day by day with the pain and suffering caused by minor accidents, enemy action and sheer disaster. Many airmen were decorated for valour and heroism, and many more died flying from its green field in our hour of need.

ACKNOWLEDGMENTS

I acknowledge with gratitude the contributions made by many people who have generously assisted and allowed me to use personal papers, photographs and manuscripts, and who have offered their own personal experiences.

Sir William F. Dickson, GCB, KBE, DSO, AFC, Marshal of the Royal Air Force.
His Grace (The Late) Duke of Hamilton, PC, KT, GCVO, AFC.
Aitken, R. S., CB, CBE, MC, AFC, Air Vice Marshal.
Hallings-Pott, J. R., CBE, DSO, AFC, Air Vice Marshal.
Beisiegel, W. K. (The Late), OBE, Air Commodore.
Down, H. H., CBE, AFC, Air Commodore.
Clouston, A. E., CB, DSO, DFC, AFC, Air Commodore.
Geddes, A. J. W., CBE, DSO, Air Commodore.
Probyn, H. M., CB, CBE, DSO, Air Commodore.
Clappen, D. W. (The Late), CB, Air Commodore.
Peck, A. H., DSO, MC, Group Captain.
Leacroft, J., MC, Group Captain.

Wiseman-Clarke, F., CBE, Group Captain.
Stansfeld, P. W., CBE, DFC, Group Captain.
Beamish, C. E., St J., DFC, Group Captain.
Ford, A. J. A., CBE, Group Captain.
Stewart, C., CBE, DSO, AFC, Group Captain.
Nesbitt-Dufort, J. (The Late), DSO, Wing Commander.
Upon, D. A., OBE, Wing Commander.
Swann, W. E., Wing Commander.
Flemming, D. M., Wing Commander.
Landrey, F., Wing Commander.
Fry, W., MC, Wing Commander.
Stewart, L. H., OBE, Wing Commander.
Blackwood, G. D., Wing Commander.
Thomas, I., OBE, DFC, Group Captain.
Jeffrey, W. T., AFC, Squadron Leader.
Kerchey, F., Squadron Leader.
McKay, G. R. S., DFC, Squadron Leader.
O'Meara, J. J., DSO, DFC, Squadron Leader.
Shipwright, A. T. K., DFC, Squadron Leader.
Hall, R. M. D., DFC, Flight Lieutenant.
Burke, P. L., DFC, AFC, Flight Lieutenant.
Batten, R. M., Flight Lieutenant.
Hartwell, D. R., Flight Lieutenant.
Baker, L. J., Flight Lieutenant.
Thompson, W. W., Flight Lieutenant.
Arnold, F. A., Major.

There are many others, sixty in fact, who have made their valuable contribution to this history by offering their own personal experiences. I convey my heartfelt thanks to them all.

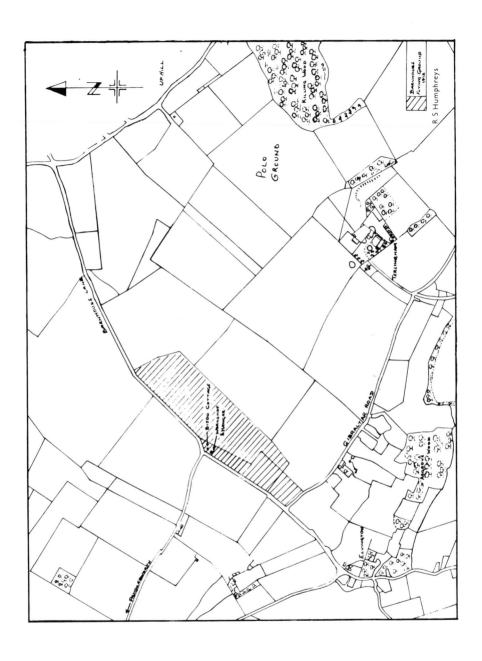

CHAPTER ONE
The Megone Experiments 1912–1914

The first flying machine seen at Hawkinge was a contraption built of spruce, welded metal tube and covered with mutton cloth. Its barking engine reverberated loudly from the surrounding trees as it bounced across the uneven turf in a frantic effort to leave the ground. These sights and sounds announced the beginning of an era that was to remain a part of village life for over half a century.

"Lift damn you — lift!"', shouted Victor Hunt desperately above the thunderous roar of the 60hp engine as he pushed and pulled vigorously at the primitive controls. Curved spars creaked while taut wires effectively distorted the mainplane to produce what was then known as warp. His feet pounded a wooden board causing a crude rudder to oscillate jerkily, sending the machine on a curvilinear course. Tufts of grass sent the contrivance bouncing and leaping and every jolt threatened to unseat him. The gyrating propeller cut through dandelion and cowslip and threw out from its axis a stream of new-mown hay.

Cap in hand, Megone the Dutchman ran after his cavorting invention waving and shouting encouragement to the struggling pilot. But what little control the would-be pilot had enjoyed at the outset had largely gone now. Wheels, cogs and chains beneath his feet rattled alarmingly. Victor searched for a quick answer to the immediate problem of how to escape before disaster struck. Fortunately a rabbit burrow which had defied detection at the preliminary field inspection saved him from any further deliberation. A wheel collapsed into the burrow bringing the machine to an inevitable and abrupt sticky end. The result was most spectacular. The propeller spun into the ground with considerable force and the flying machine literally shook itself to pieces. When the dust had at last settled Victor disentangled himself from the wreckage of wire, fabric and wood. By that time Megone had joined him and, together, they surveyed the damage.

A few hours earlier they had wheeled their invention out on to the field where the sun's rays had tightened the doped fabric areas. They had been certain then that after months of careful preparation their flying machine would actually fly. Megone had revealed to no one his intention to run the machine that day. Under the circumstances it was perhaps justified, at least the villagers were not witness to this present predicament. They had already dubbed his machine the 'Mayfly', and because of his severe countenance and commanding stature they maintained a distant curiosity. At first it had been considered an auspicious occasion when an aviator had appeared in their midst but, owing to the Dutchman's intolerant attitude, any inquisitiveness

The 'Mayfly' pusher bi-plane designed by W. B. Megone and built at the Barnhouse flying ground, Hawkinge in 1912. (A. V. Russell)

on their part was instantly rebuffed. It was little wonder that the unsociable Megone received scant sympathy when subsequent attempts to fly proved inconclusive. In any event, the flying machine had arrived although it was considered to be an unsophisticated, ugly and grossly overweight contraption.

The little flying field like others around it was part of Lord Radnor's estate and had been leased to a local farmer on which to graze sheep. Although most of the other fields were reasonably rich pasture land, that used by Megone, by comparison, was of poor quality. But whatever the inferior qualities they did nothing to hinder the eventual development of an aerodrome. In the North West corner of the field Megone had erected a large corrugated metal shed which contained the braising lamps, vices and tools needed for some of the complex workmanship. Even the massive laminated wooden propellers were made there. In the Bijou cottage adjacent to the field Megone produced designs and calculations aided by a local cycle shopkeeper called Harding, and Victor Hunt, who had answered an advertisement in the 1912 Flight magazine. Like many other pioneers at that time they were experimenting with a largely unexplored phenomena. There were few standards upon which to base their ideas. It was a hit or miss business really and, although other pioneers had been successful, much was beyond their comprehension.

Victor Hunt poses with the home-made ten feet propeller at the door of the Megone hangar.
(A. V. Russell)

The first machine constructed of light metal tube, the kind used by cycle makers, was an ugly design and, in that respect, was not a lot different to other early machines. The engine was housed in a box-like arrangement built between wing sections upon which the pilot sat. The wings and tail assembly were covered with mutton cloth stretched and glued over a spruce framework. The last known design was a collection of the best aspects of previously constructed machines long since discarded. Using the bi-plane principle in all the designs this one could be regarded as a sesquiplane with the upper wing supported by a king-post bracing method while the lower wing had a drooping dihedral configuration. There were no inter-plane struts as each wing was braced independently as a mono-wing. One very curious feature was that the rudder control wires passed through the propeller boss.

For reasons best known to himself Megone was reluctant to pilot his brainchild and had bestowed that honour, such as it was, upon Victor who, with the typical aspirations and fearless spontaneity of a true pioneer tackled it with obvious enthusiasm.

"The damn thing would never maintain height," Victor once told me, and went on, "One never quite knew if it was flying at all!"

Various engines were tested and tried out in the frame. Some of them had doubtful horsepower ratings while others were so unbalanced they shook to

13

pieces. One in particular blew its cylinder pots frequently. On that occasion Victor had to throw himself sideways onto the lower plane to avoid being struck by them.

In Megone's final design he had used the Hele-Shaw method of clutch assembly and had mentioned to Victor that with the engine de-clutched from the propeller the machine might well glide soundlessly over the heads of a foreign army in their trenches. But early taxiing trials were an hilarious spectacle. Victor suffered from bouts of hysterics when he related the stories to me over fifty years later. The heavy machine would trundle up and down the field in a series of fits and starts. The propeller, an enormous weight factor over ten feet in length was always troublesome and had frequently to be taken off and trimmed with a spokeshave. The tail assembly which embodied a unique but totally inefficient fin also carried an over-sized skid that turned the sod like a plough share. However, several modifications, more a compromise with nature than anything else, did enable the contraption to leave the ground in a series of hops and skips like some prehistoric winged kangaroo.

Designing seemed more important to Megone than actually performing flying experiments. Victor also dabbled in design work on occasions and dreamt up all sorts of ideas displaying a healthy imagination on the monoplane concept showing neat instrumentation and comfortable cockpits. Nevertheless although appreciating the imagination and rationality of his companion the Dutchman, perhaps for economic reasons, discouraged any further inventiveness. Gradually the flying experiments decreased until in September 1914, for no apparent reason that Victor could think of, he found the shed padlocked. Megone had gone. Quite naturally the Dutchman's sudden disappearance gave vent to a certain scepticism among villagers. His jaunts into the English countryside with his blue Schneider motor car and his knowledge of photography had not gone unnoticed. Everything about the man took on sinister applications. The more they thought about him after the Great War began the more they became convinced he had been a German spy, more especially when German Gothas bombed Folkestone in 1917.

But despite those stories which persisted throughout the war the pioneering spirit which had prevailed for over four years had come to an end. Soon a completely new era in aviation was to begin at this tiny flying field. The intrepid aviators, by one way or another, relinquished all claim to it when eventually Hawkinge became linked to the defence system of the British Isles.

CHAPTER TWO
Genesis of an Aerodrome 1915–1919

It was early in 1915 when the village postmaster at Hawkinge wrote to the War Office with regard to the opportunities afforded by the now deserted Barnhouse Flying Ground. By that time all sorts of war planes were being built at various factories and were being flown to the Western Front from hastily selected fields situated in the South East of England and mainly within the county of Kent. One of the first to be developed for the RFC was at Swingate near Dover in 1914, another was nearby Guston, later developed for the Royal Naval Air Service from where anti-submarine patrols were made over the Channel. Airfields were to spring up in the county virtually over night at such places as Ramsgate, Westgate, Walmer, Capel le Ferne, Throwley Wood, Bekesborne, Lympne and Hawkinge.

Although the postmaster's letter went unanswered, in September that same year military vehicles arrived at the village asking directions to the flying field. The RFC lorries were carrying personnel and an assortment of tents, field kitchens and all sorts of military paraphernalia. Within one week the RFC had removed hedges and trees dividing two of the largest fields and had altered considerably the original boundary. It was not long afterwards that unfamiliar looking canvas structures began to appear on the skyline, in the shape of three Bessoneau hangars which stood under some trees near the extreme end of Barnhouse Lane. These hangars used in the forward battle areas in France, were a quick, cheap method of aeroplane protection and the 'H' type were still being used in the nineteen thirties.

A week later the first military aeroplanes to use Hawkinge, then known as Folkestone, arrived successfully. These were the BE 2c's of No 12 squadron under the command of Major Newall, which were on route to St Omer in France. Of course there were no facilities at that time to administer to the needs of squadron personnel and so, while their aeroplanes were being refuelled, the pilots were taken to the Hotel Metropole for lunch.

The Bessoneau hangars with their flapping canvas were often ridiculed by the villagers who knew only too well of the high winds that often blustered across the North Downs. Some time later the delicate aeroplanes, bereft of their protective canvas which had blown over two hundred yards away, took the full force of wind and rain. Several machines were damaged. Because of an acute shortage of personnel additional ground staff were drafted from Lympne to help clear up the mess. Even that little operation was not without its difficulties. Fitters, gunners and armourers, all of whom had marched to the airfield from Folkestone railway station, refused to cooperate when they

One of the earliest known photographs showing the Royal Flying Corps Aeroplane Despatch Section at Hawkinge in 1916. The hangar built by the Dutchman Megone can be seen on the right, used by the RFC until 1917. (Kettle)

first set eyes on the shambles. The threat of disciplinary action aided by gallons of tea finally altered their views and reconstruction was completed without further incident.

In the following year three more fields were taken over by the RFC which extended the airfield boundary in a southerly direction towards Terlingham Manor Farm. In the spring of 1917 building began with a degree of permanency. The Bessoneaus were eventually replaced by the brick Belfast type hangar. Single story barrack rooms replaced tented accommodation and the various other structures that comprised an early aerodrome were erected. By the Autumn materials were arriving every day from the harbour and railway depots at Folkestone. The bulk of the materials, quite apart from the bricks which were being made at a brick works on the outskirts of the village, were being transported by large traction engines pulling wooden-sided trucks. These had an advantage over lorries because their weight and power at slow speeds were more suited to the steep climb up hill on unmetalled roads. However, the only serviceable route leading to the

new aerodrome was Barnhouse Lane, which unfortunately was unable to withstand the colossal tonnage of the laden machines. The large iron wheels churned the lane into a muddy mass which soon became useless and impassable. Time after time the lane had to be relaid with railway sleepers along its entire length. They too became buried beneath the mud. Eventually, through the Defence of the Realm Act, a strip of land was acquired from Lord Radnor, and a new road was cut which became known as Aerodrome Road.

Although hampered by the winter months building continued throughout on both sides of the roadway. The flow of ground staff, flying crews and aircraft being ferried to the continent increased while the building was in progress. One of the biggest projects undertaken was the building of two large hangars on the East boundary and within three hundred yards of the village. Both were completed by the end of 1918, and were originally intended to house the Handley Page 0/400 aircraft. These large bombers began arriving with the rumour that they were to invade Berlin. This however, was far from the truth for the bombing of the German capital was to be undertaken by the Independent Force of the RAF, who were to use the new H.P. V/1500 bomber. The majority of the bombers which found their way to Hawkinge were eventually flown over the Channel to No 214

The Royal Flying Corps personnel who erected the three Bessoneau canvas type hangars at the Barnhouse Flying Ground in September 1915. (Perrott)

Through the skeleton of the Bessoneau hangar, damaged in a night squal can be seen the remains of two aeroplanes. (Bass)

squadron near Dunkirk where they were used for strategic night bombing attacks in the Saar area. Those that remained were still on the airfield in 1920 and were later sold by public auction.

In order to obviate any confusion with regard to the many landing grounds which had suddenly sprung up in the South East areas a directive was issued by the Headquarters of 21st Wing, Royal Flying Coprs, on 3rd January 1917. It said in effect that all RFC stations were to be known forthwith by the actual locality in which each unit was situated. Until then the Barnhouse landing ground had been known to the War Office as Folkestone, thus it was subsequently changed to the Aeroplane Despatch Section Hawkinge, near Folkestone, Kent. It was to be so named until the end of hostilities.

It is with certain misgivings that one recalls the German attempt to bomb London on 25th May 1917. By that time Hawkinge had been in existence for about nineteen months and aircraft were being ferried to France almost continuously, but strange as it may seem, it was unable to operate in the defensive role at all. The German Gotha bombers crossed the coast between Deal and Ramsgate, heading for London. Turning away from fog bound London they flew back towards the Channel, arriving some thirty minutes later over Folkestone where they released their bombs. Over fifty women and children were reported killed. It is difficult to comprehend our inadequate defence system when there was no provision at Hawkinge to allow aeroplanes to intervene. With increased Gotha activity in the South East a squadron of fighters were eventually brought back from the Western Front, arriving at Bekesbourne in June. They did not stay long although there was every justification for them to do so.

During the Great War aircraft were made at the Royal Aircraft Factory at Farnborough and others, such as Vickers, A.V.Roe, Handley Page, De Havilland, Martinsyde, Blackburn and Airco, were made by private companies under Government contracts. Machines destined for the Western Front were flown to various Acceptance Parks in the Kent area. Hawkinge, in its role as an Aircraft Despatch Section, received many varied types: Be 2as, bs and ds; SE 5s; Avro 504s: Fe 2bs; BE 12s; FB 9s; DH 2s and 4s; RE 8s; the Sopwith Pups and Camels including the Sopwith Tri-Plane.

Because of its ability to mount a forward firing machine gun without the problems inherent in firing through the propeller, the Pusher-type aeroplane was built in greater numbers in the first stages of the 1914–18 war. These Pusher aircraft were very much slower than the conventional tractor types and with the centre of gravity almost in the middle of the machine, were found to be less stable and more prone to spins. The Vickers FB 9 (Gun Bus) was a two-seater as was the FE 2b, and both carried an observer who operated the machine gun in a forward position. The FE 12c and FE 8 were single-seaters with one machine gun operated by the pilot.

The famous SE 5, which was replaced by the Sopwith Snipe in the early twenties, was a sturdy little aeroplane coming off the production lines at the

One of the three Bessoneau hangars erected on the Barnhouse Flying field. Taken in 1917, the picture shows an SE5 and two Avro 504s. (Bass)

Lieutenant Donald W. Clappen, one of the early ferry pilots to use Hawkinge, seen here before leaving en route to St Omer in 1916.
(Air Cdre D. W. Clappen, CB)

RAE in the spring of 1917. Fitted with the 150hp Hispano Suiza engine its performance was about equal to that of the German Albatross, against which it was well matched. Later modifications including a more powerful engine gave it an even better performance and it proved to be a formidable opponent by the Autumn of 1917. During that war the 'Scout' as most fighter aeroplanes were known, handled extremely well under control of an acrobatically minded pilot and the SE 5 was no exception. Unfortunately there were few opprtunities for Hawkinge pilots to show their paces. With only a canvas belt around their waist, the pilot was not encouraged to show off. There were no shoulder straps or parachute and if a pilot did decide to perform a stunt or two it was hoped the centrifugal force would keep him glued to his seat.

The impetus for production of the SE 5 most probably came from Major General Hugh Trenchard, backed by a team of keen designers who had given the RFC some very impressive fighters. But, like most machines of that era the flying characteristics of a particular design were often hampered by a poor armament complement. In the case of the SE 5, the Vickers machine gun fired through the propeller arc, while the Lewis gun, mounted above the upper plane, fired outside the arc. The Lewis gun with or without its cooling jacket was the standard machine gun used by the RFC and had a revolving ammunition drum with a capacity of ninety rounds. There was one snag when loading the Lewis: it had to be pulled by hand down a quadrant, which proved difficult in the slipstream. Nevertheless, the SE 5 was indubitably reliable enough to be produced in great numbers and stood up to the vigorous treatment of aerial combat.

Another well known fighter ferried to France from Hawkinge was the Sopwith Camel. It was a compact 'sporty' looking bi-plane and many pilots thought it the finest combat machine ever produced. It was said to handle nicely and could out-manoeuvre almost anything in its path. With two belt-fed Vickers fitted on top of the engine cowling, firing through the propeller arc, it proved a formidable weapon indeed. By the time the armistice was declared in 1918, over 5000 Sopwith Camels had been delivered to the RFC squadrons.

By mid-1918, aeroplanes destined for France and which had already arrived at Hawkinge, were so numerous that hangar space was at a premium. Most were parked round the perimeter edges tied down with ropes passed through struts and attached to iron spiral stakes.

Ferry pilots were a motley crowd by any standard, their mode of dress was varied and confusing to the uninitiated. Some were RFC while others were RNAS personnel. Some wore two cap badges by retaining their original regimental badge. Khaki Army jackets with cavalry breeches and puttees were also worn. The only flying attire in any way consistent seemed to be either a leather flying helmet or goggles, and sometimes even goggles had been purchased from Gamages Stores, London. On the other hand ground crews retained some semblance of order in attire, the majority having been seconded to the RFC from the Royal Engineers. Their main task at the Acceptance Parks was to service aircraft before their removal to France. But slight modifications and repairs were also tackled if necessary. Riggers and mechanics swarmed over the machines checking the flying and landing wires, the control surfaces of wings and tail sections. One notable memory of those early days was the pungent smell of castor oil lubricant which seemed to invade every house in the village. Refuelling was a long and laborious job which held obvious dangers. In 1916 especially they lacked even a hand pump and each machine was refuelled by holding the two- or four-gallon cans over a large funnel placed in the petrol tank.

Each Acceptance Park possessed a 'Pool Room', from which was selected the pilot or, in the case of two-seater aircraft, pilot and gunner. Although an armourer fitted the machine gun to its mounting on the aircraft, the Observer/Gunner was solely responsible for drawing the ammunition and for seeing the weapon was in correct working order. There were occasions when bomb racks were fitted in the cockpits but usually this had already been done at the factory of origin and were mostly designed to take the twenty-pound Cooper bomb.

Control Towers were unheard of then and wireless was still at an experimental stage. Therefore the only method of signal was the Very-Light but, even so, this method was not always used.

From the perimeter fences young villagers spent the greater part of their daylight hours watching activities. In awe and wonderment they saw the huge wing span of the FE 2s, struggling against a strong wind, at times virtually motionless, hovering over the airfield like crows. Flying to the continent was totally dependent upon weather conditions prevailing at the time. Occasionally aircraft flew out over the Channel only to return later with reports of invisibility. Some lost their way and had to force land in fields on either side.

Accidents at Acceptance Parks were of course unavoidable but, fortunately, due to the slow speeds of the early machines, fatalities were rare. Most accidents were caused by bad visibility, when fog and rain turned the grass airfield into a slippery arena. It was a simple matter to remove crashed aircraft from the field. An aircraft which caught fire burned out within minutes and often became smouldering embers before anyone could interfere. Fire extinguishers did exist though not always effective.

The Acceptance Parks in France to which most aircraft were ferried were at St Omer, officially known as No 1 Aircraft Depot, Boisdinghem, St Andre, Fienvillers or Candas, the latter was known as No 2 Aircraft Depot. It has been said that a high proportion of pilots held at those depots were mostly inexperienced with only about ten or twelve hours solo to their credit. The results were disasterous, for about one-third of the aircraft flown over to France were either written off or damaged when taken to operational

A Sopwith Snipe 7F1 — F2346 — seen at Hawkinge in 1918, before the canvas hangars were dismantled. (Bass)

squadrons. Pilots at Hawkinge, although theatrical in dress, were a competent and skilled bunch and were furious at this. It was a rare occasion, however, for 'fledglings' to fly aeroplanes over the Channel from Hawkinge.

Depending on prevailing winds, the direction and force of which were constantly checked, the journey to the French-based Acceptance Parks took about an hour. During the flight the Observer/Gunner of the two-seater machines were obliged to fire their guns using the shadow of the machine as a form of target as they dipped over the waves. Obtaining a signature for the aeroplane on reaching the depot, they would then avail themselves of the many 3 ton Crossley Tenders which plied between the depots and the French ports of Calais and Boulogne. In the mid-war years, steam ships were used to convey the crews back across the Channel, but by 1918, aircraft had been made available for the return trip. This latter mode of transport although much quicker was certainly out of favour with pilot and gunner whose aspirations were more inclined towards the overnight stop at the Hotel Folkestone, Boulogne.

Before I move away from 1917, I must tell you about the story which, better than anything else I know, describes the true camaraderie of squadrons of that era. It happened on 15th March, when No 66 squadron left Filton near Bristol en route to St Omer. Commanded by Major Boyd, MC,

This photograph of a Nieuport 27 V-strutter was taken at Hawkinge in 1917. (Bass)

It was a three point landing with a difference, two wing tips and a rudder, when this Avro 504 overturned in a field near the aerodrome in 1918. (Bass)

24

they were scheduled to make a stop at Hawkinge to take lunch while their aeroplanes were refuelled. The majority arrived safely but Captain Andrews, MC, 'A' Flight Commander, was not so lucky and made an emergency landing just outside Basingstoke when his Le Rhone engine stopped. The entire Flight followed him down and landed in the field. Sometime later at his direction they took off again, but rather reluctantly. The squadron left Hawkinge in the late afternoon minus three pilots who were still sorting out various mechanical difficulties in fields en route.

When the new department of state, the brainchild of General Smuts, was established after receiving the Royal Assent on 29th November 1917, it became known as The Air Ministry, with Major General Hugh Trenchard as its first Chief of Air Staff. Recommendations made by Smuts were that the two services now operating aircraft should be amalgamated; hence the birth of the Royal Air Force on 1st April 1918.

At the outbreak of World War 1, the two air services, the RFC and RNAS, had mustered a total of 2,138 in all ranks but, by 1918, this had risen to 294,000 of whom 30,000 were pilots. Aircraft available in 1914 totalled 166, but by the end of hostilities in November 1918, over 21,000 were shown on strength. Squadrons of the RFC came to the grand total of 4 in 1914, and these had grown to over 300. The women's section of the service had grown from nought to 23,000.

Within a matter of months of the cessation of hostilities with Germany the RAF was drastically reduced from over 200 combat squadrons to a mere 30. A number of squadrons returned to the United Kingdom from France in the first few months of 1919. Some were re-numbered by amalgamating two or more units while others were disbanded a short time after moving to a home station. Hawkinge received disbanded squadrons or rather, what was left of them. In January for instance No 83 squadron, then flying the FE 2bs and 2ds, arrived and by February their aircraft were parked in an area adjacent to the Polo Ground. Considerable domestic confusion existed during that banal period when war-time skills found no outlet at all. An accumulation of non-commissioned officers, brought about by these disbanded squadrons, was a distinct embarrassment. A high proportion had served in regiments of the line before being drafted into the Royal Flying Corps. Something had to be done and a system was adopted whereby their disciplinary attributes could be exercised in square bashing. These became a daily feature of remorseless routine punctuated by kit inspections and shining parades. Pitifully, the long suffering airmen subjected to this ill-founded treatment (ostensibly beneficial to good order and discipline) thought they were social outcasts. Senior NCO's and WO's were truly in their element. Even misguided young subalterns came under scrutiny and were given an impartial 'dressing down' for not wearing the correct service cap.

The largest aeroplane ever to land at the aerodrome just after the war was a massive H.P. four engined bi-plane V/1500, which landed to refuel on 24th

This photograph of the primitive Medical Inspection Room at Hawkinge was taken in 1919. It remained in use until 1924, when a permanent brick building was erected.

(Dr Stephen Pritchard)

May 1919, having made a journey from Belfast as a commercial experiment. Such commercial experiments were a new feature in the world of aviation and Hawkinge became associated with the first of its kind.

One of the most interesting developments in air transport was the service established between England and Belgium, organised at the request of the Belgian Government and carried out by a company called Aircraft Transport and Travel Ltd. An enterprise run by a Mr Holt Thomas, it was essentially an air-lift using a number of converted DH 9 aircraft piloted by RAF personnel who flew between Hawkinge and an airfield near Ghent. They carried clothing, food and other urgent necessities required by the Belgians. This service, quite apart from the direct value of transporting essentials to a nation in dire need, was of considerable importance from an experimental viewpoint, in that it provided data for future attempts at organised air transport services.

Another 'first' operated from Hawkinge was the inauguration of the Forces Mail Service, with No 120 squadron moving from Lympne. Although carrying mail by aircraft was not new, it had been done since 1916, the first recognised mail service took place on 1st March 1919. No 120 squadron had originally formed at Lympne the year before as a light bomber unit and it was intended for the Independent Force. They moved to Hawkinge in the first months of that year and, in May, equipped with eighteen DH 9s and six DH 10s, became the first communication squadron operating from the United Kingdom.

It had been decided after the armistice to provide British troops on the Rhine with their own mail service. And so on 1st March, four DH 9s took off from Hawkinge on the very first flight carrying twenty-three bags of mail en route to Marquise in France, which had been prepared by the Royal Engineers Postal Section. The aircraft were specifically modified to take freight by converting the rear cockpit to an enclosed baggage compartment; a successful modification which was still used well into the nineteen twenties.

Prior to this a successful Military Mail Service had already been in operation in France for some time. Letters had been carried by aircraft of No 110 squadron on routes between Marquise, Valenciennes, Namur and Spar. A long distance service from Marquise to Cologne was included later and the service extended. The through service to Cologne was an unusual one in that fliers were confronted with hazards of the type not normally found on frontier routes. The first difficulty lay with the range of hills between France and the Rhine, some reaching a height of over 2,000 feet. At certain times of the year conditions around these hills were so appalling that pilots frequently experienced forced landings over terrain that was not at all suitable for such emergencies.

Wireless had been used on an experimental basis in 1918, to give means of direction (the forerunner of the Radio Direction Finder System) and it was further used to assist with weather reports and to transmit positions of pilots

The DH—E9021—pictured here was used by No 120 squadron at Hawkinge to carry mail on a service between Hawkinge and Maisoncelle, France in 1919. (Dr Stephen Pritchard)

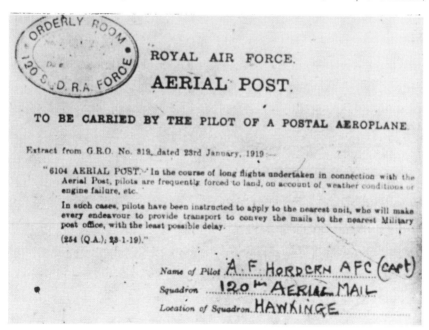

ROYAL AIR FORCE.

AERIAL POST.

TO BE CARRIED BY THE PILOT OF A POSTAL AEROPLANE

Extract from G.R.O. No. 819, dated 23rd January, 1919 :—

"6104 AERIAL POST. In the course of long flights undertaken in connection with the Aerial Post, pilots are frequently forced to land, on account of weather conditions or engine failure, etc.

In such cases, pilots have been instructed to apply to the nearest unit, who will make every endeavour to provide transport to convey the mails to the nearest Military post office, with the least possible delay.

(254 (Q.A.); 23-1-19)."

Name of Pilot A. F. HORDERN AFC (CAPT).

Squadron 120ᵗʰ AERIAL MAIL

Location of Squadron HAWKINGE

The Aerial Post identification card carried by all pilots engaged in the 1919 air mail service to the Continent. (Imperial War Museum)

28

forced down and apparently lost en route. Balloon units, light houses, pigeons and telephones all contributed to the smooth running of the service, and emergency landings grounds were situated at various points along the route.

Wireless communication was made with Maisoncelle on the afternoon of 10th April, to warn returning pilots that Hawkinge was fog bound. The message got through all right but too late as Captain Bean had already taken off. In good all-round visibility pilots usually made for the high lattice pylons situated at the RANS station Capel le Ferne, but on this occasion they were not visible at all. Captain Bean turned south until the fog thinned and the three aircraft made emergency landings near the Hotel Imperial, Hythe, from where the mail was eventually conveyed to Folkestone. A further example of pilot initiative within the squadron occurred some time later when Lieutenant Sullivan, returning from Cologne, made a forced landing at Maastricht in Holland. He had a six-hour wait before a British official arrived to relieve him of the mail bags. Despite very strong head winds an experimental flight to Cologne was made on the night of 14/15 May. Captain Barrett, Lieutenant Fitzmaurice and Lieutenant Oliver left Hawkinge at 10.15 pm in a DH 10, arrivimg at Cologne at 1.30 am the following day. They had covered a distance of some three hundred miles at an average speed of nearly 100 mph.

Normal mail flights were often the subject of light-hearted abuse among pilots as it was a pleasurable past-time, "Usually on the pretext of an alleged tiresome engine," as one put it to me, to loiter in the city of Cologne to buy, for just a few Marks, such things as pen-knives and fountain pens.

Returning from one of these 'illicit' delays a young Lieutenant was met by the duty Flight Sergeant at Hawkinge who, having looked into the rear baggage compartment, remarked to the pilot, "Engine alright now Sir?", with obvious sarcasm, and added, "By the way Sir, I see those chaps at Cologne have forgotten to unload your mail!"

Over breakfast one morning a young Lieutenant was addressed by his C.O. "Oh Pound, I see you have been detailed to fly a Brigadier to Cologne this morning. As he is extremely interested in flying would you be good enough to point out the more important towns as you fly over?"

Lieutenant Pound was a little discomforted by this, and wrote, "i had never taken the slightest notice of towns en route and in fact, I was always hedge-hopping my way across France!"

Of course aerial navigation at that time was incomparable with the sophistication attainable later. Primitive cockpit instrumentation led to errors, so the pilots flew by a kind of 'rule of thumb' technique, widely known as Bradshawing. It was by this method that young Pound usually found the twin towers of Cologne without much difficulty.

On the day in question the flying conditions were perfect for the journey. Pound took off from Hawkinge in high spirits and was able, without too much trouble, to point out to his distinguished passenger such places as Brussels, Louvain and Maastricht. By the time the cathedral city hove into view on the horizon, young Pound was as excited as the Brigadier. Pound had gained confidence with every mile and had decided that navigation was not the dreadful scourge of aviators as he had been led to believe. Revelling in the misguided belief that his passenger would, undoubtedly, praise his efforts, Pound brought the aircraft in to land with the self-assurance of a returning Scout pilot after 'bagging' a Hun. Unfortunately his normal dexterity was somewhat impaired by his excitement. The DH 9 bounced a number of times quite heavily over the tufts of grass, shedding bits of valuable machinery before it finally stood on its nose.

Pound recalled, "I turned round to see how the Brigadier had faired in this otherwise uneventful journey and was shocked to discover him sprawled half out of his cockpit with the contents of his briefcase scattered all over the field to all points of the compass!"

In July the squadron received orders to move back to Lympne and the move was put into effect on the 16th. Although conditions there were not at all satisfactory the mail service did continue for another month when they moved further North to Hendon. By 23rd August all aerial mail services ceased, largely because the Army of occupation was leaving the Rhine.

No 120 squadron had carried the mails for 130 trips out of a possible 173 and had delivered 7,164 bags weighing approximately 90 tons. In the light of these facts the mail service had been a success and, in almost every case, failure to make the journey had been due to fog. Not one bag of mail was lost and the squadron suffered no pilot losses either.

CHAPTER THREE
From Snipe to Siskin 1920–1930

In 1923, a committee under the direction of Lord Salisbury, recommended the creation of a Home Defence Force. By this time the Royal Air Force had been cut to drastic proportions both in personnel and aeroplanes. Nevertheless, it was decided, and quite rightly so, that the nation should possess an air force at least equal to others on the Continent. The only other country that held any comparable air force at the time was France, with whom we did not expect any dispute, although this was a divisive point within the Government. But like other worthwhile policies, the idea was shelved.

It was eventually decided, however, to create a new command called the Air Defence of Great Britain (ADGB) to consist of a total of 52 squadrons. Again there was a conflict of opinion between sections of the Government; some believed the whole force should be of fighter squadrons, but Sir Hugh Trenchard (Chief of Air Staff) would not agree. He, on the other hand, recommended a force of bomber squadrons and further argued that to bomb the enemy lines of communications and airfields was as vital to defence as knocking down enemy aeroplanes. 'Boom' Trenchard won the day with his plausible argument and it was finally decided to form thirty-five bomber squadrons and seventeen fighter squadrons.

This would have materialised had it not been for a Government policy introduced the following year known as 'The Ten Year Rule'. This quite incomprehensible policy was subsequenlty adopted and brought the reorganisation of our defence forces to an almost complete standstill. However, although the ten-year embargo had far reaching repercussions which were felt for many years to come, a working party devised a plan to govern the new defence force.

Based on the assumption that any likely aerial attacks of the future would most probably materialise from over the English Channel, plans to reorganise the South Eastern defences became priority. An important factor envisaged was that the air arm should be able to receive warning of attack and defending fighters should reach heights equal to that of the enemy before their arrival. Furthermore, information of both hostile and friendly aircraft should be collated and passed quickly to all sections of the defence complex. Ground defences such as anti-aircraft guns and searchlight batteries were to play an essential part in the defence structure.

The plan materialised as a belt of defence running parallel to our coastline and inland to about thirty-five miles. This became known as the Air Fighting Zone, within which searchlights were strategically placed to assist fighters at night. Outside the zone artillery was placed to defend London.

A fine picture of a No 25 Squadron Sopwith Snipe 7F1, having its engine run up outside No 5 hangar at Hawkinge 1923. (Weeks)

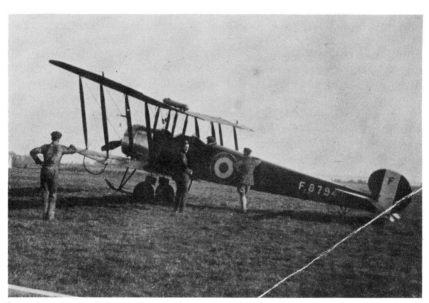

One of two Avro 504s used by No 25 Squadron for training purposes in 1924. (Weeks)

New plans and ideas were put forward and tried throughout the life span of the ADGB. Not least of these was the plan to divide the defensive belt into sections, inside which fighters could operate effectively from various aerodromes. This was achieved by cutting it into ten sectors, each having a frontal area of at least fifteen miles. Sectors to the South and East of London were allotted two squadrons each, but, in addition, three squadrons were to be based at coastal aerodromes to harass the enemy aircraft on their way to and from targets.

To parry the thrust of enemy airborne forces it was necessary to have an efficient early warning system but, even after many years of experiment, the acoustic warning devices were of poor standard. Their performance was unreliable and, in spite of extensive modifications, were still found to be wildly inaccurate. In the final stages of development concrete sound mirrors were erected at various points around our coasts. But their practical usefulness was often described as non-effective.

Hawkinge, just twenty or so miles from the French coast, became a vital link in the defence system of this country but, through subsequent air exercises, it was realised that our coastal airfields gave an unfair advantage to enemy aircraft. The defending fighters were unable to reach sufficient height to attack before enemy machines reached our coastline. This was amply verified in the summer of 1940. Although various disadvantages of the plan were minimised there was some justification in building up the fighter squadrons within the ADGB, which remained in operation until the formation of Fighter Command in 1936.

From the uncertainties and frustrations of various Government policies there evolved, in the early twenties, a new era of the fighter both in aircraft and pilots. The aerial exploits of the Great War, although not forgotten, had somehow lost their symbolic interpretation and, of necessity, pilot ambition manifested itself in the pure art of flying. Formation exercises and aerobatics became commonplace and orthodox within squadron curriculum. The silver doped aeroplanes of our fighter squadrons daubed with gay coloured stripes, chequer-board and diamond motifs, piloted by an assortment of keen and enthusiastic young men, chased around the skies. The much sought after trophies produced individual perfection in flying ability and, by the nineteen thirties, the camaraderie of the Royal Air Force fighter squadrons became legendary.

The first fighter squadron to use Hawkinge in this new peace-time role assembled and mobilised its dispersed equipment to reform on 26th April 1920 as No 25 (F) squadron, under the command of Wing Commander Sir Norman Leslie. Formerly a reconnaissance squadron equipped with the FE 2b, it had been in service on the Western Front both in reconnaissance and a bombing role. Two famous squadron members during that conflict were Lieutenant McGubbin and Corporal Waller, who gained the distinction of shooting down the German fighter ace, Immelman.

It was perhaps extraordinary that the squadron had been disbanded three months before, after returning to this country from Germany in September 1919. Nevertheless, with its initial assortment of aircraft which consisted of DH 9's and Avro 504's, and later receiving the Sopwith Snipe 7F1, it was ,at one stage, the only fighter squadron to defend the United Kingdom.

The Sopwith Snipe 7F1, with which the squadron was completely equipped by the autumn of 1920, was clearly a development of the famous Camel which had proved so reliable in the latter stages of the war. It was a compact little fighter powered by the Bentley aero-engine originally designed for the Camel and, although torque reaction brought various directional control problems these were soon overcome.

On July 3rd 1920 the first Air Display, officially called the 'RAF Tournament' organised by Sir John Salmond, took place at Hendon. The display consisted mostly of obsolete aircraft which had seen better days during the war period. Most aircraft were still covered in the drab chocolate brown dope and were in complete contrast to the silver coloured Snipe fighters of the Hawkinge squadron. The colourful squadron markings of later years were absent at this aerial diplay but the Hawkinge unit were confidently displaying flight colours on their wheel discs, propeller bosses and wing bunting. In any event, the Hendon display was a resounding success and was subsequently held annually, providing a spectacle of daring and dash.

Sir Eric Geddes, economist and industrial executive, was asked to investigate service expenditure with the result that many new projects, including aircraft design and manufacture, were shelved. However, on August 3rd 1921, exactly a month before the 'Geddes' Axe' was to fall upon the Royal Air Force, Hawkinge, pleased with its performance at Hendon, decided to have its own aerial pageant. They were able to put on an extraordinary show of aerial 'dog-fights', stunts, races round the aerodrome and a finale of bombing a mock tribal village set up in the centre of the airfield. It was all very impressive and throughout the whole demonstration only one unrehearsed mishap occurred when a Snipe somehow landed in the wrong direction and had to make various course changes to avoid hitting approaching aeroplanes. At one point the pilot looked as if he was about to jump from his machine when he narrowly missed an on-coming HP 0/400. The gyrating Snipe eventually stood on its propeller with an expensive sounding snap!

In October the following year the squadron received 'top secret' instructions to dismantle their aircraft. Large packing cases were provided in which were placed the dismembered Snipes, spare engines and parts. Personnel were given three weeks leave prior to sailing to a destination unknown. Many sought to marry. The squadron was destined for Turkey where our land forces overseas were committed to the Channak crisis. *S.S. Eboe*, converted to carry thousands of airmen lay at the Liverpool docks.

This single-seater sporting bi-plane, called 'Little Whippet', was made by Austin of 1919 vintage. Designed by J. W. Kenworthy, it was powered by a 45hp six-cylinder Anzani radial engine, cost £275 and had folding wings. It was photographed at Hawkinge in 1924.

(C. G. Gulvin)

They were to stay in Turkey for over six months, under canvas at San Stefano, operating flights in flag-showing exercises over a very wide area.

Royal Air Force participation in the Channak business led to a thinning down of our Home Defence Force and, quite naturally, additional squadrons were needed. The first of these, No 56 (F) squadron, reformed at Hawkinge on November 1st, under the command of Sqdn Ldr I. T. Lloyd. No 56 had been the first SE 5 squadron to appear on the Western Front in 1917. Two famous members were Captain Albert Ball and Captain James McCudden, both of whom were awarded the Victoria Cross.

Only one flight of Snipes became operative at Hawkinge before they left for Biggin Hill in May the following year to take up their position within the air defence system.

Meanwhile Sqdn Ldr A. H. Peck, known throughout the service as 'Bushell', assumed command of No 25 squadron in February 1923, bringing it back to the United Kingdom via the usual sea route. In residence once again at Hawkinge, the squadron was soon engaged with early warning exercises over the English Channel, when simulated attacks over the aerodrome and surrounding countryside became commonplace.

In the Autumn of that year squadron aircraft began to appear in squadron markings. The first to receive attention was the machine flown by the C.O. and it looked awful. Somehow the squadron had inherited a most dismal

Flying Officer D. A. Boyle, now Marshal of the Royal Air Force Sir Dermot A. Boyle, GCB, KBE, KCVO,AFC, is on the left of this trio taken at Hawkinge in 1925. Also in front of the Snipe of 'A' Flight No 17 (F) Squadron, are Sqdn Ldr Don with Flg Off H. R. D. Waghorn at extreme right who won the Schneider Trophy contest in 1929.   (Sqdn Ldr F. Kershey)

The 'A' Flight personnel of No 17 Squadron. This picture was taken in 1925, with one of the Sopwith Snipe 7F1s as a backcloth.

(Sqdn Ldr Kershy)

colour scheme. It had been given two unbroken lines running in parallel — BLACK. On the fuselage the two black lines ran from the engine cowling to a point aft of the roundel with two similar black lines painted on the upper surfaces of the main-plane, running between the roundels at either end of the wing-tips. Such an uninteresting colour arrangement was, fortunately, broken by the flight colours which appeared on wheels, propeller and tail fin. Additioinally, Flight Commanders' machines sported pieces of bunting tied to the outer struts.

Aerodrome Road was now a more permanent feature in the village. Along its length various anomalies had appeared in the shape of a water tank on stilts, fences, iron railings and brick walls. Trees disappeared and telephone poles were erected in their place. The aerodrome now covered a total of 177 acres and the expenditure incurred during development had reached £382,201. The largest buildings completed were the two Handley Page sheds which were of a different pattern to the usual hangars of the Belfast Bow-strut type that now stood parallel with the road.

On 1st April 1924, yet another fighter squadron reformed at the aerodrome. This was No 17 (F) squadron who received their Snipes crated from the Folkestone Junction railway station. By late May, the first assembled Flight was pushed out onto the tarmac apron and the Bentley-powered biplanes were soon being test flown over the Elham valley.

37

Gloster Grebe II — J7569 — was usually flown by Flg Off W. E. Beisiegel at Hawkinge in 1928. (Air Cdre W. K. Beisiegel, OBE)

Flt Lt 'Revver' Ford, with his Grebe J7579.
(Grp Capt R. J. A. Ford, CBE)

Under the experienced eyes of Sqdn Ldr J. Leacroft, MC, the squadron soon began to take shape, operating a rather stiff training programme which included night flying techniques. By the autumn squadron strength had reached fifteen aircraft including two Avro 504's, and the squadron insignia applied were two black lines running in pointed waves and in parallel.

In October that year, No 25 squadron became the first fighter unit to receive the newly designed Gloster Grebe. Four years before, the British Nieuport Company had been taken over by the Gloster Aircraft Company, and with it came Mr H. P. Folland, one of the leading aircraft designers in the country.

The Grebe, of wood and canvas construction, owed much to the Nieuport Nighthawk of 1918 vintage, and had a special Gloster wing arrangement whereby the top plane was of high lift which gave a better performance in a climb. Often referred to as 'the little fighter with a big heart', it was the first fighter to be ordered in any great numbers since the armistice. Powered by the Armstrong Siddely Jaguar radial engine it possessed a top speed of near 150 mph. In all some 130 machines were built including a few dual-control two-seaters for training purposes.

The Grebe, in my own view one of the most pleasing biplanes of that era, developed a most alarming fault due to wing flutter. Because of this the squadron suffered a series of accidents. Nevertheless, it was a most pleasing and delightful aircraft to fly and, as a direct result of its popularity, there was every justification for modifying the machine thus extending its useful life.

Flight Lieutenant R. J. A. Ford, recalls one of his experiences with the Grebe:

"I remember finding I was in great discomfort when diving from about 10,000 feet or more. My ears would begin to pop. I went along to see the station Medical Officer who advised me to 'Pinch your nose and blow hard man!' Evidently it was the normal remedy for such a complaint. I know that I was quite speechless and left his surgery wondering how on earth I could manage to accomplish that whilst diving at full throttle, in a machine which possessed wing flutter, clutching the control stick with one hand and my nose with the other!"

Synchronised formation flights, not forgetting the not-so-synchronised individual free flying techniques, characterised squadron activity. Flight Commanders exercised their own individual personalities and, on one or more occasions, abandoned the rule book tactics. Local farmers became immune to the noise of low-flying aircraft and also, by necessity, became expert in the identification of certain pilots whose cheery wave of the hand they most often acknowledged by shaking a clenched fist.

It is a marvel that accidents were so few when one considers the daring show of individual airmanship that was sometimes witnessed. The tranquillity of meadow and country lane was often shattered by snarling radial engines. Fowl and cattle leaped this way and that as screaming Grebes

No 25 Squadron pilots on a battle flight at Odinham. Kent in 1926. Sqdn Ldr A. H. Peck, DSO. MC, on extreme right. (Grp Capt R. J. A. Ford. CBE)

shot between cow shed and barn. There was the occasion when a Flight of Grebes brought their machines within a few feet of a combine harvester which was busily disgorging corn stooks some little distance from the aerodrome. Pitch-forks and caps went flying as the labourers flattened themselves against the stubble. They little realised that in about fifteen years time they would be doing the same thing to save their own lives.

But squadron life was not all fun. One of the most memorable sights of those bygone years was biplane formation flying. This had been developed to produce team confidence and had, from the outset, provided a proud showpiece of skill and individual ability over the years. This professionalism did much to bring a high standard of morale to the RAF. The whole concept of this type of flying is a matter of pure concentration and discipline on the part of pilots who, above all, must keep the correct spacing between the aircraft and unhesitatingly follow the leading machine. The whole formation becomes as one as each pilot concentrates on the aircraft on his immediate left with an eye on the leader and ignoring the ground.

Sqdn Ldr Peck's fine and accurate performance before His Majesty King George V, at the 1925 Hendon Pageant, remains, to this day one of the best contributions ever made by a highly efficient squadron in the art of flying. Although no one thought of using smoke canisters to emphasise the manoeuvre, the Grebes, in impeccable formation, under the direct control

40

A unique photograph taken inside No 2 hangar at Hawkinge showing the Grebes of No 25 Squadron. (Air Cdre W. K. Beisiegel)

of His Majesty by wireless, executed a new manoeuvre called 'The Prince of Wales Feathers'. Code-named 'Mosquito', the squadron C.O., leading two sections of four aircraft, climbed into a half roll while the other two sections made climbing turns outwards. This same manoeuvre with all its precision, pomp and swank, greeted the arrival of No 56 squadron at the beginning of the Army exercises held at Andover the following month.

In March 1926, No 17 squadron watched with interest the arrival of the Hawker Woodcock fighter to replace their efficient Snipes. Designed as early as 1922, by Hawker's Chief designer, Captain Thompson, it was in some respects similar to other aircraft, possessing a two-bay wing configuration. The early machines, powered by Jaguar engines, displayed many alarming features such as sloppy rudder action and the dreaded wing flutter. Struggling designers contrived to alter the performance of, what must have been even then, an outdated aircraft. Later Woodcocks with a new engine and single-bay wing sections gave a more satisfactory performance. Wing flutter was still evident however, although to a lesser degree. The squadron flew them with mixed feelings. Traditionally built of wood and fabric the Woodcocks succumbed to the uneven surface of the airfield and structural weaknesses such as main-spar, strut and undercarriage failures, were the main causes of aircraft grounded for repairs.

Later versions were fitted with night flying equipment and carried as armament two Vickers machine guns, synchronised and conveniently placed either side of the fuselage within easy reach of the pilot.

It was during one of the nightly excursions when No 17 squadron were

41

exploring the delights of nocturnal flying that a Sergeant Pilot Thomas came to a rather sticky end. Thomas was about to land from an easterly direction when suddenly the flare-path disappeared from his view. He was by then over the village and committed to make a landing. He thought, at first, he would undershoot the grass and end up on someone's roof so he 'blipped' the engine for more power. The undercarriage caught a hedge bordering the Polo ground. The resulting crash was somehow muffled by the mist. But to the half dozen or so airmen tending the flare-path there was no mistaking the mishapen, tangled mass of metal that was slithering towards them over the dew-soaked grass. Sergeant Thomas dislocated a shoulder.

Throughout the year the two Hawkinge based squadrons dictated the usual RAF policy of peace-time training, both by day and night. Villagers were usually thankful when the normal day operations had ceased by 5 o'clock. But the hourly drone of night exercises, by no means a labour of love for those taking part, was even less acceptable. Despite the inconvenience many were thankful, in days when thousands of unemployed were on hunger marches and strikes, that the aerodrome provided the life-blood to their families.

The well established pattern of training included air-firing, camera gun practice, pin-pointing, wireless practice and aerobatics. The air-to-air firing practice was naturally as close to the real aerial combat as peace-time would allow, using the camera gun. Air-to-ground firing was usually carried out at the Lydd ranges where splash targets were put to great advantage near the Camber sands. Later, and especially in the mid-thirties, air-to-ground firing took place at the Hythe School of Musketry ranges where large coloured steel plates were erected as targets.

Pin-pointing practice was, as every flyer will agree, the most important if not essential navigation exercise. Pilots were to realise later in their service how much they owed to this form of practice. In possession of a special kind of skeleton map upon which were inscribed the bare details of an area over which they would fly, they ranged over the Kentish countryside, picking out their obscure details to fly to a strict schedule. Accuracy in identification, compass courses and speed, were essential to the success of the exercise.

The cumbersome Woodcocks of No 17 squadron left Hawkinge for Upavon, in October. They left behind two rather conspicuously crumpled machines which were eventually absorbed into the newly formed storage unit that was now working in the Handley Page sheds.

The Wessex Area Storage Unit, to give it its correct name, began operating early that year, and was eventually to occupy most available hangar space. Initially the unit only accepted new aircraft direct from the manufacturers which were flown in and then stored to await delivery to bomber squadrons in the Wessex area. As the bomber squadrons were to re-equip with a particular aircraft type, they were checked over and brought up to flying standard. Collection was carried out by the actual squadron

The crashed Gloster Grebe of Plt Off Purvis, whose death was mentioned in the House of Commons during a debate on flying accidents. 1926. (Gulvin)

making the change over and, inevitably, their old and sometimes worthless machines were left behind for disposal. The majority of the Virginias, Victorias, Hyderabads, DH 9s, DH 10s and Vimys, had quite often seen better days and serious defects were frequently discovered on inspections. It was no wonder that many pilots flying them found the mess bar an essential haven!

This collection of antiquated machinery was broken up into component parts and eventually disposed of, either to scrap dealers or sent to other storage sections. There were occasions when a complete aircraft was sold to a private buyer.

Maintenance work in all aspects of aircraft preservation techniques was carried out by both RAF and civilian personnel, who also had close liaison with various modification squads who arrived from time to time from the aircraft manufacturers. Sea air mists were not ideal conditions in which one would normally seek to store aircraft. Nevertheless, the unit became quite an efficient and highly organised section of RAF Hawkinge.

On December 9th 1926, during air-to-ground firing exercises, the squadron lost one of their young pilots in a fatal accident. A Flight of Grebes had been diving towards their target, in this case a series of circles cut into the turf near the centre of the airfield, when Flg Officer Purvis lost control of his machine. With the engine screaming in a near power dive the Grebe

43

crashed into a hollow near Terlingham Manor Farm, where it burst into flames. Working close by was Albert Daniels who, without regard to personal safety, rushed to the pilot's aid. He cut the harness and dragged the pilot clear of the inferno, sustaining severe burns to hands and face. The ill-fated flyer, a nephew of Sir John Gilmour then Secretary of State for Scotland, had died instantly.

News of his death reached the House of Commons and was announced during a debate on the growing number of fatalities in the Royal Air Force which now totalled 83 since the end of hostilities in 1918. Concern was expressed, not only by Mr Baldwin the Prime Minister, who naturally deplored such accidents, but also by Sir Samuel Hoare, the then Air Minister, who remarked that they had not yet discovered a remedy against flying accidents. But the Minister took the opportunity to inform the House that every possible precaution was being taken, and further, that the standard of training, inspection and supervision of aircraft and airmen, was the highest in the world.

Albert Daniels received a suitably inscribed gold watch for his gallant rescue bid, which was presented to him by Air Vice Marshal H. R. M. Brooke-Popham, on behalf of the Air Council, in the following January.

Fields to the North of Aerodrome Road, used for troop training exercises in the Great War, were finally sold to Folkestone Corporation in 1927. Almost immediately a cemetery was established there. It was not at first considered an encouraging sight from the air but, as far as memories will allow, its presence instilled a traumatic, if not sobering, effect on certain pilots whose flying was considered somewhat flamboyant.

The irrepressible silk-scarf image existing throughout the Royal Air Force in the mid-twenties was, in most respects, an extension of the social background from which the majority of Officer material emerged. Fresh out of school or college, these ambitious young men entered the halls of RAF Cranwell and, by so doing, had joined one of the most exclusive of 'clubs'. Passing out from Cranwell, they were not usually sent to the squadron of their choice, but where their special abilities would be best served. Their subsequent arrival and initiation at squadron level became an inspired and somewhat emotional experience.

The idiosyncracies of senior staff were varied , and there always seemed to be a mixture of a strict disciplined code of conduct somehow coupled with a kind of cultural benevolence. Blooding of young pink-faced fledglings was inevitably a mild affair, for there was no combat to sort out the wheat from the chaff. Ultimately their keenness in striving to perfect their flying ability induced a form of friendship with their elders, who at best still regarded them as 'low life'.

In direct contrast, the non-commissioned officer pilots, regarded by many as the backbone of operational fighter squadrons, were treated with a certain awe, and were indiscriminately respected by all ranks.

This Fokker VIIa of the Dutch KLM Airline made an emergency landing at Hawkinge in 1928. Incidentally, this aircraft was later destroyed at Schipol Airport by German bombs on 10th May 1940. (E. Daniels)

The rudimentary principles of flying, both theoretical and practical, learned at Cranwell, were now over for two new arrivals recently posted to Hawkinge. Their delight at being selected for one of the most famous fighter squadrons was, however, short lived. To their utter astonishment and dismay, a Sergeant Instructor was given the task of finding out if their flying ability could be proved beyond doubt.

Each fledgling demonstrated his individual flying expertise in the dual-Grebe, to the satisfaction of the instructor who gave little verbal encouragement to either. But, with circuits and bumps over they were later encouraged by the C.O. to gain valuable experience on cross-country flying. These aerial jaunts, away from daily squadron routine, afforded a mode of relaxation, making up for the lack of social activity that older members of the squadron enjoyed. Their turn was to come but now, on twenty-one pounds per month salary and with mess bills averaging between £12 and £15 per month, visits to the Folkestone Majestic Hotel were all too infrequent. Unobserved and occasional spasmodic wireless contact was made with the aerodrome, the young pilot officers ranged far and wide, each flight an extension of the last. But for the inconvenience of the occasional forced landing, they gained valuable experience and insight that no lecture could demonstrate.

Destined to play cricket for the Royal Air Force, in the summer of 1928 W. K. Beisiegel took every opportunity to fly to various matches. Likewise Charles Beamish, the third in age of four famous brothers, made full use of this opportunity to attend the Irish Rugby season.

The advantages of being a single squadron station at that time also had disadvantages. Young subordinates had extra responsibilities thrust upon them which usually amounted to Officer in charge of the airmen's mess, Motor Transport section and Orderly Officer duties which seemed to come

Gloster Grebe No J7412 of No 25 Squadron had collided with another during a battle flight on 17th February 1928. The pilot, Walsh, baled out. (Gulvin)

Plt Off Beisiegel, hands on hips, waits for his Grebe to be put on an even keel after it overturned in a heavy landing. (Gulvin)

round with rapid frequency. Flt Lt Ford was quite agitated to discover that his stint at Orderly Officer coincided with an impending farewell celebration. Ford, whose thirst was only secondary to his friendship for the posted Harcourt-Smith, exchanged duties with a teetotal member of the squadron who, quite unbeknown to him at the time, was to take on more than he bargained for.

On the day in question every available officer accompanied their C.O. With bayonets firmly fixed, the impeccably turned-out guard stood to attention as the cavalcade of privately-owned motor cars swept past the guard room. The popular Harcourt-Smith was to remember this day, as indeed were the rest of No 25 squadron. A bewildering state of affairs arose. During the speeches aboard the ferry at Dover, punctuated here and there with a stiff toast, the pilots rose to their feet for the umpteenth time with glasses poised. Then suddenly a sobering hush fell upon the assembly when someone discovered the ferry had slipped anchor and was now heading for France.

The Captain of the ferry was informed immediately but, although indicating his sympathy, refused point blank to turn about. And so, confined to the saloon the squadron personnel made the most of their predicament and continued their celebrations until Calais was reached.

Some six hours later the slightly dishevelled and inebriated squadron alighted at Dover. The Duty Officer at the aerodrome had received a hastily arranged telephone call from the ship. His feeling of utter dejection when he at first realised that he was in sole command of one of His Majesty's Aerodromes later gave way to one of alarm. The truth was so incredulous he hardly dared to think about it. He began to invent plausible excuses, should someone of high rank appear asking for the C.O. In the event, he was spared from making any misrepresentation of fact. The humorous aspects of this little escapade veiled the more serious connotations, which only began to be considered when everyone involved met in the mess bar that evening.

Since the fitting of the 'V' struts in 1926, there had been few serious accidents but, on 17th February 1928, two Grebes collided in mid-air and in poor visibilty. Both machines were climbing through cloud in typical battle formation when the tragedy occurred. Pilot Officer Walsh suddenly found his machine in a spin. He tried recovery procedure only to find his rudder not answering. A quick glance revealed no tail section at all. Walsh scrambled over the side and pulled his rip-cord. Flt Lt Watson in the other machine failed to leave his Grebe which spun into the ground. Walsh was later rescued from the telephone wires in which he had become entangled at Crete Road East, about two miles from the airfield.

The subsequent enquiry held a week later excluded any question of mechanical failure. The squadron was proud of its mechanical expertise, under the eagle-eye of an inspired Flight Engineer who fussed over squadron aircraft as if they were rare time-pieces.

Sqdn Ldr W. H. 'Porky' Park, C.O., No 25 Squadron in 1927.
(Grp Capt R. J. A. Ford, CBE)

A Siskin IIIa — J8878 of No 25 squadron. The Siskin was the first service fighter to use an all metal construction with fabric covering. (Wg Cmdr F. Landrey)

One of the experimental parts of the Grebe seemed to be the wireless equipment. Those early wireless sets were quite unpredictable, cumbersome and powered by heavy, awkward accumulators. Communication beyond fifty miles was indeed a most fortunate occurrence. But Flt Lt 'Joe' Stewart, the jovial and stalwart 'sparks' of the squadron, devised a means of improving reception by packing the valves with cotton wool! It seemed to work.

Flt Lt Stewart did much to teach the pilots the correct use of the wireless equipment and, was also enthusiastic in other extra-cockpit activities during off-duty hours. He founded the 'Wobbly-Wheelers Cycling Club' which he led from time to time in sorties to local hostelries. The wonder of it all is that they always found their way back to the aerodrome!

Squadron Leader Park fell ill and he was succeded by the senior Flight Commander, W. E. Swann, whose first duty was to take the squadron to Hendon on October 11th, for a repeat performance of their display sequence for the benefit of the Sultan of Muscat and Oman. The finale over, Swann prepared to leave the display area but, to his utter astonishment, a new fighter prototype, flying at very low level, actually flew into the Royal Enclosure. Luckily the Sultan was taking refreshment in the nearby club house and escaped injury.

'Porky' Park, Squadron Leader, a great personality at RAF Hawkinge, died suddenly after an emergency operation. His successor, Sqdn Ldr L. G. S. Payne, arrived to command the squadron on January 1st 1929. Even before he arrived it had been rumoured that he had close associations with various theatrical people on the London stage. Quite naturally the squadron hoped they would find him visited by female lovelies from the current shows. But in this theory they remained hopeful but disappointed. Payne became Air Correspondent to the Daily Telegraph during the late thirties and was also the author of a book called 'Air Dates'.

In July 1929, the squadron re-equipped with the Armstrong Whitworth Siskin IIIas, taking them to Sutton Bridge in the following month for the annual training exercises.

The Siskin had already been in RAF service for the past four years and was really another outdated fighter. Too large, heavy and docile they had a rather disappointing performance. The true Siskin definition was Sesquiplane, it having a high upper plane with a rather short lower wing plane. Dropping a wing or putting a wing in were two terms often used in Siskin squadrons when accidents were often due to the ineffective lower wing. A wooden skid was provided under each lower wing tip but it proved useless in preventing accidents. Tarmac critics were given additional pleasure by these unofficial manoeuvres which were often caused by strong cross wind currents.

One good feature of the Siskin was its robust undercarriage. Powered by a 450 hp Siddely Jaguar air-cooled engine, the Siskin did not live up to the

The Siskin crash on a Folkestone sports field, in which Sgt Pearce lost his life.

(E. Daniels)

manufacturer's claim of 156 mph at sea level. The top speed attained at Hawkinge was about 10 mph less. With fabric covering a metal framework, the first fighter in RAF service to use that type of construction, it possessed two Vickers machine guns synchronised to fire through the propeller arc. Of course, the Constantinesco synchronising firing mechanism was standard equipment throughout the RAF, usually referred to as 'CC', and operated by cables from the pilot's control column.

Especially suitable for day and night operations, the Siskin fitted with flame damping exhaust stacks, carried in addition to wireless and small bomb racks, full night flying equipment that incorporated cockpit heating. This latter innovation was not only beneficial but also a potential killer.

Sergeant Pearce, a most able and competent pilot, was lost to the squadron in circumstances which can only be described as sinister. The battle flight had taken off in impeccable style and was climbing out to sea above Folkestone, when Pearce's Siskin was observed to leave formation in a gradual downwards direction. Such ill-fortune to befall one of the squadron's most gifted pilots was very distressing. The only obvious conclusion reached by the Court of Enquiry was that the luckless Pearce had been overcome by carbon monoxide fumes from a leak in the aircraft heating system.

CHAPTER FOUR
Bi-plane Phobia 1930–1938

At the dawn of a new decade the aerodrome, with or without an adequate early warning device, still remained an important link in our defence system and relied upon an outdated air arm for much of the 1930s.

Even the National Press, during this period, revealed the inadequate defences of the country, and wrote of the risks of an aerial attack on our cities. In considering such an appalling event, just twelve years after a war, the significance and absolute necessity of adequate defence was quite apparent. Somehow little was learned from the German Gotha air raids and it was, perhaps, unforgivable of those in Government office who failed to realise the potential devastation of modern air power.

However, it is true to say that by the mid-thirties a slow and sometimes ponderous Ministry did make furtive attempts to put things right. Their first step was to submit new aircraft specifications to the aircraft industry, but these fell far short of modern requirements. In the main, aircraft designers were sticking faithfully to the old and well established principles. Despite this biplane obsession, fate took a hand in the creation of two revolutionary monoplane fighters which were to fight side by side in one of the greatest air battles of all time.

As press reports of threat and rumour of war increased from the Continent, so did our efforts, until finally, we saw fit to camouflage our silver biplanes and our new eight-gun monoplanes as our squadrons were put on a war footing.

But before it was to take place, Hawkinge was to see many changes both in personnel and equipment. The first change involved Sqdn Ldr Payne, who relinquished command of No 25 squadron. He was succeeded by the popular Sqdn Ldr R. S. Aitken, DSO, MC, who had received his Wings at Swingate Downs in August 1916. He took command of the squadron on 6th February 1930, putting the pilots through their paces for that year's Hendon Pageant.

It was about August when Aitken, who had been a flying instructor as early as 1918, took his squadron of Siskins up to the usual 18,000 feet ceiling on a routine battle climb. He eventually became concerned by the apparent sluggishness of his particular aircraft but continued to climb. Black spots began to appear on his goggles but he dismissed it as splashes of oil. Later it became a case of the blind leading the blind, for, although unbeknown to Aitken, the rest of the squadron pilots were experiencing the same discomfort. After a while he decided enough was enough and brought the squadron down. Alighting from his machine he was immediately set upon by the other pilots wielding their map cases with gusto. It transpired that the

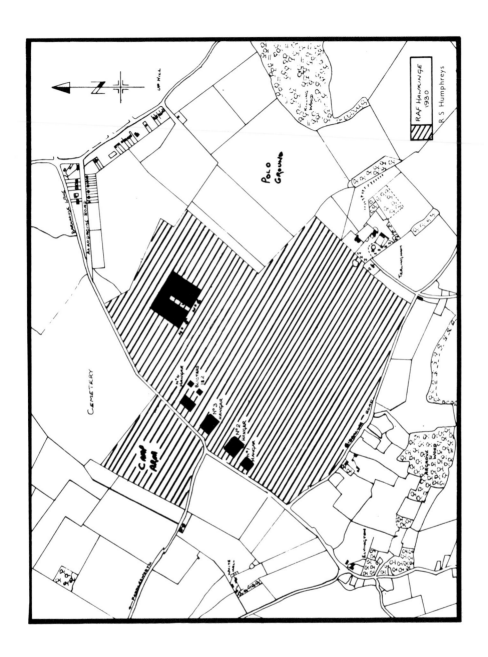

RAF HAWKINGE
1930

R S Humphreys

52

C.O.'s altimeter had stuck, and that 22,000 feet had been reached without oxygen!

Stories abound of forced landings by pilots due to a variety of reasons. Mechanical failures did exist, contrary to the boasts of successive Flight Engineers. Pilot error was not uncommon but the inevitable sea mists caused havoc, and were certainly instrumental in one incident which befell Flt Lt Keary. Gale force winds had subsided and the sky became a mass of scudding clouds leaving visibility somewhat inpredictable. Keary took off to test-fly his recently overhauled Siskin. Climbing above the cloud base into bright sunlight, he was soon lost in that ecstasy of flight that every pilot recognises as his world. Stimulated by the rhythmic purr of the big Jaguar engine, a 'Will-o'-the-wisp feeling took over. This illusion soon vanished however, when on returning, he found the aerodrome area completely covered by mists.

A peculiar and disturbing feature of those swirling mists lay in their density from sea level to above 8,000 feet. It was a dangerous meteorological phenomena of immense concern to the Hawkinge squadron, and for any other come to that. Low on fuel, Keary's plight multiplied when he was told by wireless that an area of some thirty-five miles radius was affected and lay under a thick blanket of fog. A combination of skill and luck brought him to earth in the middle of Army Bell-tents on Dibgate Camp near Shorncliffe.

Mentioning the Army brings to mind the Army affiliation exercises which were always a feature of squadron training and, annually, they gave various low-flying demonstrations to troops on the Small Arms School ranges at Hythe.

On August 8th 1930, the squadron lost a Siskin and pilot during similar exercises held at Falmer near Lewes, Sussex. This particular demonstration had been to show how fighter aircraft would attack troop concentrations whilst they were on the march. Three Siskins of 'C' Flight were used and, on their final simulated attack, were reforming from very low-level when Sergeant McNair, his engine throttled back, banked to starboard and waved to the troops. His flying speed was obviously too low and this error of judgment cost him his life. The Siskin ploughed into a field and broke up.

Another accident, although of no particular consequence to the squadron, always brought a smile to the lips of people relating it afterwards. For some obscure reasoning known only to the pilot, a DH 9a, destined for the Storage Unit, made its landing approach between two hay-ricks which stood near to the airfield boundary. At little more than about 40 mph, it got caught up in some wire which had been strung out between the ricks. The wire arrested the aeroplane which flew into one of the hay-ricks and burst into flames. The amusing sequel to this needs some believing, but I have been assured it is true. Apparently the fire picket ignored the pilot who, covered in hay and with flying goggles askew, was taken for a scarecrow!

Sqdn Ldr Aitken left the squadron for H.Q. of the ADGB in October. He

Sqdn Ldr H. M. 'Daddy' Probyn, C.O., of No 25 squadron 1930, prepares to lead the squadron on their weekly battle climb in his privately owned Widgeon.

(Air Cdre H. M. Probyn, CB, CBE, DSO)

Wapiti — J9836 flown by Sqdn Ldr The Marquis of Clydesdale, then C.O., of No 602 (City of Glasgow) Auxiliary Squadron 1931.　　　(The Duke of Hamilton, PC, KT, GCVO, AFC)

Although usually considered a docile aircraft to fly the Siskin was often upset by gusty cross winds.   (Wg Cmdr F. Landrey)

later became Air Attache in China until 1940, and later still was A.O.C. to No 60 Group (RADAR) until 1943.

His successor was Sqdn Ldr H. M. Probyn, DSO, who was affectionally known throughout the service as 'Daddy'. He later commanded the Royal Air Force College at Cranwell during the last war.

Probyn became very proud of No 25 squadron. Its neat and precise formation flying was universally admired. He was also the proud owner of a light blue Westland Widgeon aeroplane which had come fifth in the 1927 Kings Cup air race. Newcomers to the squadron were often irritated by the appearance of the Widgeon at very close quarters during formation practice. They were even more irritated when Flight Commanders throttled back to enable the light aeroplane to catch up! They soon learned the reason and discovered, to their surprise, that their intrepid C.O. was actually filming their progress, camera in one hand and control column in the other!

An accomplished horseman and a member of the East Kent Hunt, Probyn invariably carried out his camp inspections on horseback, presenting a fearful figure to the not so industrious airmen, but it must be said that he possessed a benevolent personality.

Squadron personalities at that time included Victor Beamish, then 'B' Flight Commander who later flew in the Battle of Britain. Another was Flt Lt Hancock, 'C' Flight Commander, who wore the DFC, a rare decoration in those days, won for gallantry whilst he was serving on the North West Frontier. A newcomer was Fl Off Nesbitt-Dufort, who during the Second World War was to be associated with the Special Operations Executive squadrons, something which required a special kind of courage.

During the summer months the aerodrome received Auxiliary squadrons who were combining their ADGB exercises with their summer camp activities. One in particular is always remembered, No 602 (City of

Glasgow) squadron, who at one time were flying the Westland Wapiti, under the command of the Marquis of Douglas and Clydesdale.

Their tents were usually pitched near the petrol dump area and sometimes encroached upon the airfield where, occasionally, aircraft ran amok. Both village and station would be rudely awakened at the first light of day, about five o'clock in the morning, when the squadron padre walked between the tents blowing his bagpipes. "They called him a man of God!", someone once said.

Wandering airmen were, it seems, a special breed. Either walking or riding cycles, they appeared oblivious of aircraft landing or taking off. Without thinking or caring of the hazards they wandered everywhere and always at the wrong moment. Special notices were put up to discourage this trend but the most effective method practised was to chase them with low-flying aircraft! The airfield had a slight dip in the centre with a gradual slope to the East boundary, almost a saucer shape although it looked quit flat from the air. It was deceiving, to say the least of it. One could stand near the East boundary with your back to the village and watch an aircraft almost disappear to the West as it taxied away from you. At night with a strong cross wind blowing it could be quite unhealthy to the unwary pilot.

Both the auxiliary and the permanent squadrons took to the air in a show of strength in the annual air exercises that year. Day and night all kinds of aircraft ranged over the southern counties representing an imaginary Continental Power called 'Blueland' who were to attack London. Aided by the Observer Corps, searchlights, sound indicator units and intelligence sections, the 'Redland' fighters would attempt to defend the metropolis. Crew briefing went on for hours and the multiplicity of rules and restrictions were, to a large extent, a manifestation of ill-defined ideas. Minimum height restrictions was one of the first considerations because the public at large failed to appreciate the importance of aerial defence. It had to be 5,000 feet over London and 2,000 feet elsewhere. Navigation lights had to be switched on for fighters and this brought groans from those pilots affected. Special aircraft crammed with scribbling umpires flew alongside the formations taking notes on who had been shot down. Bombers selected as 'shot down' however, continued to their target in ignorance where they were attacked once again!

It was very confusing and, when the whole episode ground to a halt, almost everyone had decided that communication was the answer to all the problems. Something was achieved of course. Fighters had got off the ground in record time and bombers found their targets without much trouble. Interceptions were extremely good too. Something had been achieved as in all previous operations and in any case, it was the best they could do until the invention of Radar.

On 10th August the C.O. had the unhappy task of attendiing an inquest on Pilot Officer Dennis G. Vaughan-Fowler, a young pilot detached from No

Frequent visitors to Hawkinge in 1930 were those interested in gliding who used the Officers'
Mess facilities. Left to Right: Herr Krause – Susie Lippins (Belgian) – Master of Sempill
Gordon England – Herr Kronfeld – Manager of Midlands Bank – Flt Lt L. H. Stewart – Herr
Magasuppe. (Leo Stewart, OBE)

41 squadron. Vaughan-Fowler had asked to take part in the search-light
tattoo being held on the Folkestone football ground. His Siskin, decked out
with dozens of coloured electric light bulbs suddenly developed an engine
fault as he made his approach for landing back at the aerodrome. With no
power at all the Siskin turned a complete somersault as it touched down and
immediately burst into flames. There was nothing anyone could do to help
the pilot who had over 234 hours solo flying to his credit, including six hours
night flying.

During the fourteen months stay of Sqdn Ldr Probyn, the Channel
Gliding Club came into existence. Even before he arrived there was a lot of
interest in gliding techniques and design, which had occupied the minds of
squadron members. Flt Lt Stewart had stimulated public interest by writing
to the local press. A Corporal Manual had already designed and built a
glider the year before. Serious design inaccuracies had resulted in some
hair-raising attempts to get the contraptions to fly. The usual method had
been to use a motor car for towing. On one occasion, when the C.O. was
away from the station, a chocked Siskin was used to blast the glider into the
air. But it failed. I believe the Flight Engineering Officer had something to
do with it as the Jaguar engine began to overheat! Non-powered flight took
the curl out of Flt Lt Fox-Barret's moustache (an appendage about which he
was justly proud) when he was salvaged with difficulty from the wreckage of
a home-built glider that had plummeted to earth from about forty feet.

Corporal W. B. Manuel of No 25 Squadron built this replica in 1929 of the Octave Chanute glider that hangs in the London Science Museum. (W. B. Manuel)

Later, with the help of a generous donation from Lord Wakefield, a hangar was erected on a piece of ground adjoining the aerodrome. As a result of Stewart's plea in the press, local interest produced new designs. One glider built in the village could only be released by taking part of a wall down in the owner's house. He seemed unperturbed by this. Club meetings were held in the Queens Hotel Folkestone, and in July 1930, a demonstration of gliding took place near Crete Road East, Capel. Enthusiasts included Herr Von Kronfeld, the famous Austrian pilot who, in his own machine, the Wren, had earlier that year set up height and endurance records of 10,000 feet and 93 miles.

In September 1931, two Siamese Air Force Lieutenants were attached to No 25 squadron for training. Both were average keen pilots. Tragedy occurred during air-to-ground firing practice one day when one of the machines stalled whilst making an evasive move to avoid another aircraft. The Siskin spun down and crashed on Caesars Camp. Lieutenant Sujiritkul was killed instantly.

In the following year a spate of accidents occurred. The first was in January when a Siskin was written off strength having slewed round on take-off. The pilot, Flt Lt S. Rasanandar, the second of the two Siamese, sustained only minor injuries. In February Sgt Pilot Hobley was injured when insufficient power on take-off put his Siskin through a hedge. Perhaps the Siskins were becoming worn out. By the end of the month, however, the pilots were delighted to receive the new Hawker Fury Interceptor fighter.

The Fury was to become the pride of the Royal Air Force. Developed from the Sidney Camm designed Hawker Hornet, it looked and handled like a real fighter with regard to speed and manoeuvrability. It was a fine sleek

The Hawker Fury I Interceptor — K2078 is seen here outside No 2 hangar ready for a test flight. 1934.   (Wg Cmdr D. A. Upton, OBE)

biplane with an in-line Rolls-Royce Kestrel engine of 525 hp driving a Watts wooden propeller. Top speed was approximately 207 mph and it was capable of climbing to 10,000 feet in just over four minutes. Fully aerobatic, the Fury flew like a dream and was the envy of many less fortunate squadrons although, strange as it may seem, the aircraft did not experience widespread service in the RAF. This was in some respects, due to the Bristol Bulldog fighter, another new design being produced in great numbers. However, the unquestionable superiority of the new Interceptor over many other types persuaded the Air Ministry to equip the three most forward based fighter squadrons, Nos 1, 25 and 43, with them.

Sergeant Pilot 'Max' Upton, was one of the first to try his hand at flying the new Fury in squadron service. 'Max' was a most capable and experienced pilot and he recalled the occasion vividly.

"I remember when I climbed into the deep cockpit through a door panel on the port side I practically disappeared. But I soon found the seat winding handle and wound myself up to windshield height. The instrumentation, if I remember correctly, was fairly standard and the spade grip on the long slender control column had the Vickers machine gun triggers attached. Beyond the windshield was the usual ring and bead sight with the Aldis sight alongside it and both were fixed to the polished engine cowling."

Sergeant Upton liked what he saw and beckoned the Hucks Starter to engage its goose-necked gearing to the propeller boss. With the engine firing on all cylinders he waved chocks away. The Fury gained speed with every yard as Max opened the throttle.

"She came alive," Max told me, and went on, "I could feel the control surfaces funtioning beautifully — she only needed a mere touch and she answered perfectly."

As the other squadron pilots were waiting their turn back on the tarmac, Max completed a few mild turns but nothing as brash as a loop or anything at all that looked aerobatic.

Over the village roof tops he closed the throttle and selected petrol mixture to rich and trimmed aft. With the two blade wooden propeller just visible he let the speed drop away to about 70 mph then gradually brought the control column back into his stomach.

"She settled like a bird," Max said. "You know — she bounded along the grass on her long stroke oleo legs like an ostrich. I thought she was the ultimate in fighter design then — in fact I held that view for some years until I tried the Spitfire."

The new Furys were soon painted in squadron insignia and, for the first time, the 'Hawk on a Gauntlet' was painted on the tail fin. Mind you, some so-called talented airmen had tried to apply the insignia free-hand, but the C.O. soon had a template made and issued instructions on the correct colour scheme.

Getting used to the Fury proved a turning point in squadron tactics. Previous ideas were abandoned or modified as it was much faster than the old Siskin. Targets loomed up in the gun sight at a speed that gave less room for marginal errors. The squadron worked hard to devise new methods for attacking bombers in the annual air exercises. The Interceptors usually attacked in threes, one machine on either side of the target with the Flight Commander coming from beneath. Split second timing was required to give the best results. They usually attacked, re-formed and went in again as the bombers, most often one of the Hart variants, maintained formation relying on their cross-fire gunnery to save them from destruction.

However, the term Interceptor was, to some extent, misleading. It could be imagined that this particular type of aircraft would be at the throats of the enemy before crossing our coastline. This was the role envisaged. The decision to design, and indeed produce aircraft of this type, was taken after the 1927–28 Air Exercises, when it was discovered that our existing fighters were unable to climb rapidly enough. The main consideration therefore, was to create an aircraft capable of reaching its ceiling height rapidly. Endurance was not considered essential and so the sleek Hawker Fury evolved.

Probably due to our indifferent Sound Locator Units, it was found in the 1932 Air Exercise that to throw our Interceptor fighters into the bombers whilst they were over the targets was, in effect, a more profitable way of defence. And so the Interceptors became key members of the ADGB, and were in constant training to better their performance, both in actual interceptions and take-off times. At one stage they reached the phenomenal two minute take off.

No 25 squadron Fury team practicing their 'tied-together' formation flying for the 1934 Hendon Air Display.   (Daily Express)

With considerable insight into the needs of a fast growing service the Air Ministry launched a two-year building programme at the aerodrome in 1932. Two large barrack blocks were the first to be constructed around the original drill square. A mortuary was built, incredibly small by any standard, and one wonders if the planners ever envisaged that it would, in years to come, house briefly before interment, the bodies of airmen slain during some of the greatest air battles ever to be fought in the skies over England.

At Hendon this year Sergeant Pilot 'Jock' Bonar excelled with a fine performance of aerobatics to delight the crowds. When Bonar left the squadron later that year he became a flying instructor at the CFS, where he was awarded the E.G.M. for saving the life of another instructor. Later still he joined Sir Alan Cobham's famous flying circus.

The squadron Hart Trainer collided with a Fury on 17th September. Flt Lt A. E. Clouston was the pilot with Fg Off Dunworth as passenger who was on instrument tests. Dunworth broke a few bones but Clouston was uninjured. Clouston later became famous for breaking the world record for flights of endurance to the Cape, Australia and New Zealand.

Squadron Leader A. L. Paxton took over the squadron on 28th February 1933. He led the squadron aerobatic team through their paces for the First Empire Air Display which, for some unknown reason, was held at the former R.N.A.S. station at Capel le Ferne. This was the time when Adolf Hitler's rise to the Chancellorship fused the old and the new Germany

Sqdn Ldr 'Tony' Paxton briefing the display team. From left to right:—Sqdn Ldr A. Paxton – Flt Lt C. R. Hancock – Sgt D. A. Upton – Sgt M. Pearson – Flt Lt K. B. Cross – Flt Lt Douglas-Jones – Flt Lt Blackburn – Flt Lt A. E. Clouston – Flt Lt M. Daunt.

(Wg Cmdr D. A. Upton, OBE)

Pilots of No 25 squadron on the steps of the Officers' Mess at Hawkinge, 1932.
Back row: Fg Off L. F. Brown, A. E. Clouston, T. A. Head, R. G. Harman, R. G. Arnold, Plt Off T. A. Hunter.
Middle Row: Fg Off's H. St.G. Burke, R. P. Garnons-Williams, G. P. MacDonald, Sqdn Ldr E. G. Bryant, MBE, Fg Off C. B. Hancock, DFC, F. P. R. Dunworth, N. Daunt, J. Nesbit-Dufort.
Front row: Fg Off A. E. Douglas-Jones, K. B. B. Cross.   (Flight)

62

together. In April that year the new German Air Ministry was formed with Goering installed as Air Minister. It was at this point we were to hear the first rumblings from the Continent. Soon every member of the German Armed Forces was to take the oath, the oath which was the rock of Nazi power and obedience which led to the German Military Forces carrying out acts of oppression.

In lighter mood I must tell you about the Kestrel engine. It was a fine piece of machinery with but one major fault, the carburettor stopped working when the aircraft was inverted. This was a feature still evident in Rolls-Royce Merlin engines a decade later. An example of this tiresome fault is illustrated in an expensive, but otherwise unrewarding, crash of a Fury, piloted by a young man imitating skills he had not yet mastered. Like every other pilot in the squadron, he was captivated by the exhilarating, delightful Fury. His feelings of exhibitionism overcame his better judgment however.

He executed the first of what was to be three rolls whilst approaching the aerodrome boundary. Airmen were gathered in small groups at the hangar doors during a break in routine. Their attention to the cavorting Fury was not unduly attracted even when the second roll was perfectly executed, although by this time the aircraft had lost considerable height. Whilst attempting the 'Hat Trick' the petrol-starved Kestrel gasped and died. The now inverted Fury slowly settled to the ground, its threshing propeller losing momentum. The dust had hardly settled over the mis-shapen biplane when the luckless pilot released his cockpit harness. He descended even further to the ground head first!

In what might be called typical sports-day style, lounging airmen suddenly bolted out onto the airfield. But their progress was interrupted by a Warrant Officer. Within the comparative seclusion of the hangar he instructed them in tact which was to seal their lips for months to come. With only one civilian witness at the subsequent Court of Enquiry, the young pilot was given the benefit of the doubt.

Another Fury was slightly bent when a Sergeant Pilot tipped his machine up on its nose at Lydd, during Army Co-operation exercises. But a more seriously battered Fury was written-off squadron strength in March. Flt Lt Nesbitt-Dufort had taken off with the remainder of the squadron for their weekly battle climb but his machine only reached about twenty feet before the engine suddenly cut out. Still over the airfield the pilot was left with little choice in making a reasonable landing. Immediately in front of him was either the ammunition dumps, the cemetery or an old oak tree. He remembers choosing the lesser of the three evils!

Seconded from the Royal Engineers, Major Arnold, in charge of the rebuilding programme witnessed with some displeasure the burning of No 4 hangar. It all came about when the special reserve squadron, No 504 (County of Nottingham) based then at Hucknall, brought their Hawker Horsley bombers to the aerodrome for their summer camp. About a dozen

The burning of No 4 hangar on 7th August 1933, caused by a crashing Hawker Horsley of No 504 (County of Nottingham) squadron. (Grp Cpt F. W. Wiseman-Clarke)

This aerial photograph taken in 1933, was from a Siskin IIIa of No 25 squadron piloted by Sgt Plt D. A. Upton. (Wg Cdre D. A. Upton, OBE)

The Hawkinge Fire Tender and crew outside No 5 hangar 1929. (R. Marwood)

arrived followed by over one hundred airmen and at least two dozen officers. Their rather intensive training included some twenty-five hours flying for every gunner on the unit. They flew their air-to-ground gunnery practice at Lydd and used the Leysdown ranges near Sheppey for bombing practice.

Early that morning a flight of Horsleys had left for the bombing ranges at Leysdown. Some two hours later, Flt Lt Hartridge, making his landing approach from over the village roof tops, momentarily froze. The Rolls-Royce Condor engine had spluttered and then stopped. With over two and a half tons of aeroplane to handle and no engine power, Hartridge guided the machine to a perfect three-pointer onto the single-bay roof of No 4 hangar, where upon it rolled miraculously to a stop at the brick parapet above the doors. Whilst pilot and navigator scrambled to safety down a hastily placed ladder, the fuel, escaping from punctured wing tanks, trickled down inside the walls and ignited. Inside the hangar were six Blackburn Dart aircraft in storage. Airmen dragged clear a brimming petrol bowser, its paint peeling in the searing heat and likely to explode at any minute.

The Air Defence of Great Britain squadrons were now increased to thirty-five finalising the original plan outlined eight years before. The Auxiliary squadrons were converted to fly fighters leaving the newly appointed regular units to form as bomber squadrons. Air Ministry specifications for a high speed, high performance monoplane fighter gave birth to the famous twins, the Hawker Hurricane and the Supermarine Spitfire. This decision of course, although inevitable, had far-reaching consequences beyond the imaginativeness of our politicians. Four decades hence the 'twins' are revered in prodigious immortality.

Motor Transport section of No 25 squadron, outside No 1 hangar in 1934.　(R. Marwood)

Gates and doors were flung open to the Public in May the following year for the Empire Display, when Flt Lt Clouston and Dainty, brought gasps of admiration from over 2,000 spectators as they performed dazzling aerobatics. Flt Lt Daunt took off on one wheel and Sqdn Ldr Tony Paxton led his nine Furys tied together with coloured bunting. It was a spectacle not to be missed. Each Fury had a length of bungee (round rubber formerly used to form shock absorbers) fixed at the top and bottom of the rear inter-plane strut. Two lengths of stout cord, about twelve feet in length, were then tied to the middle of the bungee and the ends of the cord were joined by about six feet of kite cord with a breaking strain of near ten pounds. Finally, flags were sewn to the thick cord at intervals.

Display sequences of the 'tied Furys' usually followed the same pattern beginning with nine aircraft already tied together in three flights of three, taking off in line abreast, turning on 360° and climbing to the display level of 2,500 feet. A loop was then performed in a 'V' of nine, easing out into three flights of three forming line abreast. Next came the barrel-roll with each flight in line abreast formation, before reforming into the V formation. Two loops followed this in a tightly knit formation then there followed the spectacular prince of Wales Feather, where each machine broke away in a different direction. Sometimes and especially during practice for the Hendon pageant, flights of three machines landed with bungee still attached and with cords unbroken. All in all it was usually well executed, showing the skill of airmanship. It earned the pilots high praise indeed.

Few members of the public knew of the preliminary rehearsals of those

66

As Secretary of State for Air, Sir Phillip Sassoon was a frequent visitor to Hawkinge. This DH Puss Moth — G-ACLW, was Sir Phillip's first private aeroplane and is seen here at Lympne with Sgt Plt 'Max' Upton at the controls. (Wg Cmdr D. A. Upton, OBE)

fine performances, which took place in the weeks before the full flying drill. Those who worked at the aerodrome watched in astonishment as dungaree-clad pilots pedalled cycles recklessly around the parade square to the shouts of the C.O., and Flight Commanders.

Paxton left the squadron and Sqdn Ldr W. E. Bryant, MBE, took over. But the 'elite No 25', never changed, they always lived up to their well earned reputation. Aerodrome telephone wires hummed and buzzed when irate civilians complained about low-flying aircraft. Flying under telephone wires required a certain skill and courage which he civilian population failed to appreciate. Officially such low flying was frowned upon by both the Air Ministry and squadron commanders. Nevertheless it was this spirit of dare devil achievement which proved our salvation in the years ahead.

There was the occasion when, fearing a head-on collision with a Fury which seemed to be flying on the railway lines between Westernhanger station and Sandling Junction station, the train driver braked so hard that passengers were thrown to the floor of their carriages. Distraught passengers complained bitterly to the station master at Folkestone. Fortunately, most complaints were ignored, for the Secretary of State fo Air at that time was Sir Philip Sassoon, whose private aircraft was usually flown by a member of the Hawkinge squadron.

The combined tactical rehearsal of defence strategy began this year in July, and was no better or worse than those held previously. Only the

This DH 90 Dragon Fly — G-AEDT, was the second of Sir Phillip Sassoon's private aeroplanes also piloted by Sgt Plt 'Max' Upton.　　　　　(Wg Cmdr D. A. Upton, OBE)

Observer Corps, searchlight and sound locator units, both regular and territorial forces, were given the opportunity to use their respective skills. The Air Ministry directive sent to all units taking part stated rather laconically: 'Live ammunition will not be used'. Someone at the aerodrome had added 'Thank God' in ink. Perhaps because the aerodrome was designated an enemy airfield for the exercise!

The annual exercises for 1934 began on 23rd July, and the Furys of the Hawkinge squadron left for Hornchurch to become part of the defence force named Northland. Restrictions were stifling in the extreme and any achievements attained from this particular training exercise were purely nominal. Certain regulations were enforced to avoid unnecessary risks, especially when aircraft were, once again, flying over London. Fighter pilots were severely handicapped. Bomber units on the other hand, were allowed to use the cloud base along their pre-arranged route to their targets, but the fighters were not. Navigation lights were required to be switched on during the whole night operation and even during daylight hours the fighters had to give way to avoid forcing the bombers to change course. In addition, the frustrated fighter pilots found they were forbidden to attack by diving from above or behind, and further, that not more than one fighter was to make an attack at the same time. They were also advised not to engage an opponent within three miles of its target!

The three-day exercise went off without a hitch and no one took any notice of the misguided individuals complaining of the noise over London. There were a few confusing reports from Umpires and one or two emanating from Folkestone. Refuelling techniques were rather slap-happy affairs when everyone, from the A.O.C. down, was only concerned with the quick turn around of fighters to beat the two-minute take-off time. The net result was a series of explosions in a street in Folkestone. Biplanes were usually refuelled by three machines being placed in a triangle over the petrol filling points. Speed was essential and an airman would stand above the aircraft on top of the main plane with a hose. As soon as one petrol tank bubbled over and regardless of the risks involved, the hose would be quickly transferred to the next. The result was that aviation fuel spilled and found its way into the storm drains. Hundreds of gallons went this way unnoticed until a manhole cover suddenly blew off in Folkestone High Street. Samples taken by the authorities later proved quite potent. It was some time before the source and cause of the explosions was discovered.

In July 1935, Hawkinge became a Station Headquarters and Sqdn Ldr W. F. Dickson, who was in command of the squadron, became the first station commander. By then the aerodrome was well laid out with each building served by well kept paths along which had been planted shrubs and flower beds. It was typical of most RAF aerodromes in that peaceful era but Hawkinge in particular became a magnificent fragrant landscape where the perfume of flowers mingled with the pungent aroma of petrol and oil. At one stage the solid looking hangars were whitewashed and could easily be seen from the French coast. The grass airfield was cut with meticulous care, each mowing was made with guardsman-like precision. It was a sight which would have delighted the crowds at Wembley Stadium. It was no coincidence either for Mr King, an ex-Grenadier guardsman who had seen action in France during the Great War, took pride in his work.

In August the Fury Is were replaced by the updated Fury IIs. Super Furys they were sometimes called. They had a more powerful engine, wheel spats, a slight increase to their wing span and height but retained the sleek lines of its predecessor reaching 233 mph at 1,000 feet. Paintwork to control surfaces had been abandoned by then so the usual tricolour markings were not appled to the rudder.

At lunch time on 3rd November, a convoy of heavily laden lorries turned into the gate between the hangars and stopped outside No 3. Within the hour fifteen Silver Hawk Audax biplanes of No 2 Army Co-Operation squadron had arrived from nearby Manston. Airmen were directing stores everywhere and, by four o'clock that afternoon, both aircraft and stores had been neatly stowed away out of sight. Local farmers threw their hands up in despair when they heard another squadron had arrived.

The seven-looped knot family crest of Sir Hereward Wake was painted on

A fine picture of the Super-Fury Interceptor at Hawkinge in 1937.
(Sqdn Ldr W. T. Jeffery, AFC)

This fine picture of K1995 aptly illustrates the 'message Hook' system of retrieving messages from the ground. This particular Audax was the first production machine to be flown on 29th December 1931 by Hawker's Chief Test Pilot, P. E. G. Sayer. It was one of 40 aircraft built to Specification 7/31 using the Kestrel 1B engine. It crashed at Hawkinge on 13th August 1936.
(Rex Puttee)

just about every item belonging to the squadron. The squadron crest was the usual six-pointed star of Army Co-Operation units but, in addition, a black triangle, a relic of the First World War, was painted on aircraft fuselages.

No 2 squadron was originally formed in May 1912, and became the first RFC unit at Farnborough. At the outbreak of the First World War they were moved to France to provide reconnaisance for the British Expeditionary Forces. The unit was disbanded soon after the armistice but was reformed on 1st February 1920, later seeing service in Shanghai in 1927, flying the Bristol Fighter. The squadron can boast two VCs from the First World War period, 2nd Lt W. B. Rhodes-Moorhouse, who was in fact the first ever VC, and 2nd Lt A. McLeod.

The function of an Army Co-Operation squadron, right up to the Second World War, was to work in close liaison with ground units of infantry, artillery and tanks, keeping them informed of what lay ahead. If the ground forces were unable to attack certain positions owing to the heavy concentration of the enemy, then the A.C. squadrons were called in to intervene. They would attack the enemy with bombs and machine guns, blow up bridges and railways and attack enemy strongholds.

The work of the pilot was more complex than that of his counterpart in fighter and bomber squadrons. It was both varied and exacting even to the point of self-defence for usually they flew alone or in pairs. The pilots were all of commissioned rank, and were selected especially for this type of work, most of their training having been carried out within the squadron after completion of a three months' course at Old Sarum, Wiltshire. At the School of Army Co-Operation where instruction was given in signals, arms and military tactics, they were given a good, sound grounding, before being sent back to their squadrons. Training continued at squadron level and annual tests were held for each pilot in subjects such as firing the Vickers or Lewis machine guns, rifle and pistol shooting, map reading and photography. The standard required for an A.C. pilot was of the highest, needing special qualifications in practically every aspect of military flying. It follows quite naturally that the aircraft also were selected for their versatility.

The Hawker Audax was a development of the famous Hart, an aircraft frame which offered an almost unlimited range of variations for all military duties. It possessed good handling characteristics, easy maintenance and a fairly good speed and range performance.

It was a two-seater biplane with the 'N' struts and single-bay type wing section but, unlike the fighter, had two large exhaust-pipes, one on either side of the fuselage, extending back to, and just below, the rear cockpit. The performance in terms of speed was not on a par with the Fury as they were designed for different reasons. Bombs were either carried under the wings or in the fuselage. Releasing them varied but usually a cable release system attached at one end to a clip and the other to a handle in the cockpit was used. The bomb sight was by no means a sophisticated piece of equipment, but it was a highly sensitive and delicate instrument which allowed automatically for air speed, wind drift, and altitude.

Training of bomb-aimers was facilitated by means of an ingeniously designed invention called the Vickers-Bygrave Bombing Teacher. This apparatus set up at Hawkinge was in a large wooden tower, where instruction took place in near total darkness. A projected image representing the ground, reflected on a white floor, afforded a most realistic representation of actual flight. Between the projector and the image a platform, complete with bomb sight and navigational instruments, was suspended for use by the observers. The projected image was moved to represent the motion of the ground as seen from an aeroplane, and was able to produce the effects of banks and turns and to simulate the effects of wind direction and air turbulence.

On May 23rd 1936, over 3,000 people attended the Annual Empire Air Day, which sadly ended in tragedy. Flying Officer Ashton, a Cranwell cadet, with L.A.C. Simpson as his airgunner/observer, were crew of an Audax of No 2 (A.C.) squadron who, in company with two other machines, had just completed a mock attack on a wood and cardboard fort set up in the middle of the airfield. This kind of mock attack had been done many times before, both at Hendon and Hawkinge.

Dummy bombs were dropped onto the fort as suitably dressed airmen in flowing white sheets ran amock, shooting off blank cartridges from disguised service rifles. It was perhaps too realistic. Timid children ran to their parents as pandemonium reigned over the whole proceedings. The three Audax in line astern swept out over Folkestone and turned yet again for their second run. The leader, Flt Lt Andrew Geddes, pushed his control stick forwards and the biplane put its nose down. The speed built up to around 140 mph. The other two machines followed. As Geddes left the aerodrome boundary bombarded with cardboard particles from the blank anti-aircraft shells, fired in his direction, he was closely followed by the second machine. But the third machine struck a 33,000-volt electric cable near Holywell, with disastrous results. Ashton and Simpson died instantly.

It was a disaster all the more significant because of the mood of the audience. One minute they were excited and the next stunned. Their mood changed to one of gloom. They began to leave the aerodrome quietly in small groups. Cooling aero-engines stood in silence while airmen stood watching the black smoke curl above the tragedy.

The 1936 disclosure that Germany's Air Force was now at a staggering 2,500 aircraft caused a major Royal Air Force reorganisation. The old A.D.G.B. was abolished and four new commands created — Fighter, Bomber, Coastal and Training Commands. By the following year the expansion scheme had moved so fast that each new scheme overtook the previous one before completion. Our defence policy, however, gradually materialised and in two years, when German troops entered Austria causing

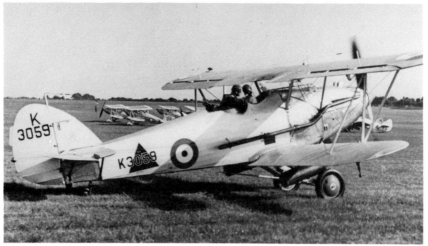

Hawker Audax — K3059 of No 2 (Army Co-operation) squadron, taxiing to take off position behind Furys of No 25 squadron. Both units were taking part in the 1937 affiliation exercises.
(Rex Puttee)

yet another European crisis, our air staff were beginning to secure even better results. New units were being formed but, as was the case with previously formed squadrons, some were to be equipped with obsolete aircraft making their effectiveness as a modern fighting unit highly questionable.

Outwardly such reorganisation was slow to reach coastal squadrons although Hawkinge was transferred, within No 22 Group, to Fighter Command. There was a reshuffle of personnel and one of the first to go was the C.O. of No 25 squadron, who had been promoted to Wing Commander. His place was taken by Sqdn Ldr H. H. Down. The new and up-to-date officers' mess was nearing completion when the first contingent of No 601 (City of London) Auxiliary squadron arrived for their summer camp. A party of Observer Corps, using some rather basic instruments plotted the arrival of a dozen or so Hawker Demons, which flew at varying heights and speeds.

Rivalry between regular and Auxiliary squadrons was always intense and most often high spirited, and the pilots of No 601 were no exception to that rule. Their clandestine activities became legends. Sports cars, driven by an assortment of rich young men, assailed the perimeter defences at the aerodrome in the dead of night to sabotage anything on which they could lay their hands. On one occasion a raiding party equipped with soda-syphons, invaded the officers' mess with great success. Another retaliatory onslaught, when the squadron were based at Lympne, concerned the use of service aircraft to make a bombing attack upon Hawkinge.

Sir Phillip Sassoon's home at Port Lympne, was used by the RAF during the Second World War.

(Wg Cdre L. H. Stewart, OBE)

The last private aeroplane of Sir Phillip Sassoon, a Percival Q6 (G-AFFD)was usually piloted by a member of No 2 (AC) squadron. As Sir Phillip was the honarary Air Commodore of No 601 (County of London) Auxiliary squadron their unit insignia was carried on the fin of the Q6. A coiled Cobra of Gold was a personal emblem. (Air Cdre A. J. W. Geddes, CBE, DSO)

Officaldom put its foot down hard on that little game and service machines would not be used for such games in the future. The following day saw a number of privately owned aircraft, in perfect formation, peeling off over the aerodrome and dropping bags of flour, soot and even toilet rolls. On that occasion wind direction was south-westerly and consequently they made their attack from this quarter. This happened to be one of the few occasions when the cemetery nearby resembled a spectacular surrealist's canvas. Tombstones were unfortunately besmattered with a concoction of soot and flour and trees in the immediate area became festooned with government paper. In the evening sunlight they took on a pink hue. But this wonderful exhibition of colour failed to pacify the ecclesiastical gentlemen residing in Canterbury. They were not amused. The Hawkinge fighter squadron came in for its share of criticism from the church soon after that episode.

Droplets of oil and petrol often fell from inverted fighters engaged in aerobatics and had gone unnoticed when they fell on village roofs. The result was that fatigue parties spent long hours scrubbing tombstones.

Outdated Very cartridges from the armoury bolstered the heart of what was to be the biggest Guy Fawkes bonfire ever seen at the aerodrome. Bits and pieces borrowed from the storage unit, due to close that month, were arranged like some huge flying contraption from one of Jules Verne's novels. At its core were hundreds of feet of training film used in the Eagle cameras. The effect, as you can imagine, was spectacular and explosive. As multicoloured flares shot into the night sky the fierce heat cracked windows in the nearby officers' mess.

Even the Christmas party that year went off with a bang. Father Christmas was to appear suddenly in front of curtains while a puff of white smoke was to add credibility to his entrance. Somehow the mixture of magnesium and other chemicals had been overdone. The blue touch-paper was lit while Father Christmas adjusted his cotton-wool beard. There was an enormous flash. Paper-chains and all manner of decorations disappeared and the portly gentleman, whose impressive entrance had been assured, was momentarily blinded. He picked himself up from the floor to the accompaniment of children's screams. An airman was seen to leave the building in hysterics.

On the occasion when the Army Co-operation squadron left for Friday Wood, Colchester in February 1937, on their annual camping stint, they had trouble with their pet goldfish. Stores and equipment usually went by road of course, but the pets were to fly. Everything seemed alright until the aircraft was climbing over London.

"Better not climb any higher Sir!" shouted the gunner to his pilot, and on whose lap rested a large glass bowl containing half a dozen prize goldfish. Take off had been tricky as vibrations of the aircraft caused water to slop over the edge of the bowl. Now, evidently, the fish were suffering the 'bends' hence the frantic cries from the rear cockpit.

"Fish are blowing up like balloons Sir!" added the gunner, who was hoping to receive an order to jettison the whole caboodle over the side. But no such luck. The aircraft descended to a more reasonable height and the marine life deflated. Operation for the return journey became more scientific when a cover was provided for the bowl.

Impressed with the successful formatiom flights of the Italian General Balbo, in the first half of the thirties, Flt Lt Andrew Geddes, then 'B' Flight Commander of No 2 squadron, approached his C.O. for permission to organise his own special 'Balbo'.

"We would gain valuable navigational experience Sir," Geddes explained, and went on, ' . . . and of course we could study the problems inherent in long distance flights away from our home base."

"It seems a very good idea, Andrew, but where do you propose to go?" Sqdn Ldr Opie asked.

Blue eyes twinkling, Geddes opened a large piece of paper which outlined the proposed route, overnight stops, heights and speeds and a host of other data essential to the mission.

"First leg to Catterick, Sir, then on to Leuchars, Inverness, John O'Groats, Abbotsinch, then across the Irish Sea to Aldergrove via West Freugh. Next we fly to Sealand, Filton, Lands End, Old Sarum and the final leg home Sir!"

"You seem to have done your homework," the C.O. remarked. "When do you propose to start?"

"Thought the 19th April would be suitable Sir!" replied the Flight Commander, undoubtedly pleased that the C.O. was not being difficult.

"I also thought," Geddes went on, "we might have some visual by-products of the trip, Sir — oblique photography, taken of the three aircraft over principal points, by the fourth air gunner. There is some spectacular scenery en route, Sir — such as the mountain ranges of the Cairngorms, the magnificent Loch Ness, Ben Nevis and of course Lands End."

Not wishing to dampen such ingenuity the C.O. agreed.

And so on the morning of April 19th, four specially prepared Audax machines of 'B' Flight took off on their first leg to Catterick. Andrew Geddes was more than usually careful about overnight maintenance, fuel, compass swinging preparations and navigation, map reading and appreciation of weather forecasts and reports. There were no direction finding techniques and facilities available in those days to aid crude cockpit instrumentation. Radar was along way off. Geddes realised more than once during the three-day flight how much depended on his own experience.

Unfortunately the flight planned from Leuchars in Fife, to John O'Groats then back to Leuchars was foiled by deteriorating weather. It became quite tricky. He cut out John O'Groats altogether, and instead made for Nova, Iona and then Abbotsinch near Glasgow. The meteorological office at No 1 FTS Leuchars provided a rather miserable forecast of a depression coming

The three Audax of 'B' Flight No 2 (AC) squadron over Loch Ness during the long distance flight in April 1937. (P. W. Stansfeld)

in from the south west, which unfotunately would give fuel problems if the wind increased since the route was mainly into the south west airstream.

Over Inverness and before actually reaching Nova, the barometric pressure began to lower rapidly. Geddes decided to turn a little short and went down on the Great Glen, past Fort Augustus and Loch Arking and then on to Fort Willam. Difficulty was experienced in getting a photograph of Ben Nevis owing to thickening and lowering cloud. The front actually caught them before they reached Oban. From Fort William it was under the clouds all the way via Loch Linnie, Connel Bridge, Loch Elive, Pass of Brander, Gladich, Glen Aray, Inverary then sharp left to Dundarave Point.

In line astern the four Audax shot into Hells Glen, aptly named for it looked like a vast letter V with massive rocks towering on either side. To make matters worse the top was covered with cloud. Only the bottom half of the V could be seen to guide the leader through the sheer rock face.

They emerged on the other side like highland geese and reformed in echelon starboard to cover the distance to Loch Goil. As Loch Long passed beneath them they could see on the skyline Gourock and the aerodrome at Abbotsinch. After touch-down Geddes checked his fuel left in the tanks and discovered there was only enough for ten minutes flying!

The remainder of the Balbo was, by comparison, uneventful, except the final approach to Hawkinge. Looking down on the sprawling town of Basingstoke, the flight leader unwound the 120 feet trailing aerial with its lead weight on the end.

"Hello Hawk this is Balbo Leader — are you receiving me, OVER?"

"Hello Balbo Leader this is Hawk — receiving you loud and clear, OVER!"

Geddes received a rather disappointing weather report. The dreaded Hawkinge hoodoo he called it and it seemed bent on spoiling an otherwise successful exercise. He acknowledged the report but continued on course, determined to see for himself. Twenty minutes later the three Audax machines with the fourth tucked in behind were over the aerodrome. Visibility was just as the watch office people had predicted. It was appalling, even the large hangars were not visible at all, let alone the rest of the airfield. Below the wives and friends stood in groups waiting the flight's return. Andrew Geddes knew the disappointment if he decided to land elsewhere. He waited for thinning cloud, circling the aerodrome at about 5,000 feet, until at last he could just distinguish the bulk of one or two hangars. He quickly lit the Holst flares on the lower wing tips to reduce the possibilty of collisions. The other pilots followed suit and it proved to be a most impressive and quite dramatic arrival. The Balbo had been great fun for all concerned enabling initiative and flying expertise to flourish in days before Air Traffic Control or Radar had been invented.

Another example of open-cockpit flying without the benefits of modern science occurred some two months later. That was one of the few occasions when the Mess Bar was opened against the normal rule of 'no alcohol to be consumed until the hangar doors were closed'.

The occasion of an eighteen aircraft near-miss over Folkestone will be etched on their memory for ever. The bar steward remembers it as the day when the greatest quantiy of brandy was diepensed in any one day at Hawkinge. He recalled the extraordinary sight of pilots gesticulating with their hands to explain the attitude of their own aircraft during the split seconds when each pilot was trying to avoid a collision.

It began as a rather sedate exercise of the two squadrons in their respective formations of nine aircraft in typical V, flying over an imaginary military parade. It had been a pleasant morning's flying with both leaders listening out for their individual instructions on different frequencies of their wireless. The sun had shone earlier giving a warmth to the proceedings, but suddenly, as often happens at coastal aerodromes, orographic cloud swept in from the sea, it began to rain and conditions were decidedly bumpy. Both leaders automatically opened up their squadrons to about a span to make it easier for the outside aircraft. Normally on these exercises the V was flown absolutely with aircraft 'tucked-in' with wing-tip overlap.

And so it happened that nine Furys in line abreast, carrying out their last instruction were flying out to sea while, at the same time, nine Audax in line

Led by Sqdn Ldr H. H. Down, the nine Fury IIs reach Herne Bay on the Kent coast.
(The Aeroplane)

abreast, carrying out their last instructions, were flying inland. Both squadrons were at the same height!

Eighteen aircraft were now on a collision course at little more than 800 feet above sea level. At less than one hundred yards distance, eighteen pilots thought the day of reckoning had arrived. Rich and wholesome vocabulary accentuated the rapid movements of rudder bars and control sticks. Four machines, the two outer aircraft of each squadron, zoomed up into the vertical stall turn simultaneously and they were fortunately high enough for the inevitable spins not to be fatal. The remainder scattered in all directions of the compass.

Both C.O.s, visibly apprehensive, climbed down from their machines on the aerodrome and stood side by side, each with his own thoughts. They stood in silence both contemplating the disastrous effects of the remains of their squadrons scattered over Folkestone.

Eventually, to their great relief, one by one, the aircraft returned to make their landings. The atmosphere was electric. That is, until the order was given — "No more flying today — the mess bar will be open at lunchtime!"

At the Empire Air Day the following month the usual high standard of flying ensued with spins, loops, dives and low flying. There were of course

The 1937 No 25 squadron display team. Left to right:—Sgt W. T. Jeffrey – Sgt Haine – Sgt Walley – Flt Lt Cameron – Sqdn Ldr H. H. Down – Flt Lt Nedwill – Plt Off Lonsdale – Sgt T. Blackburn – Sgt Aggett.   (Sqdn Ldr W. T. Jeffrey, AFC)

the formation flights and this year in particular it was the A.C. squadron who flew a very impressive formation in the figure '2'.

There was one very amusing incident recalled. Members of the public, numbering nearly 4,000 that year, were invited to give flying instructions to an aircraft by wireless. Not many people availed themselves of this opportunity, most were timidly shy of the huge microphone, but one highly excited individual took up the challenge. Phrases such as 'Will you turn left, please', and 'Would you be good enough to make a dive, please', not only sent the signals section into hysterics, but caused the hapless pilot innumerable difficulties.

Participation in public relations could prove costly as the squadron were to find out.

The Fury had changed direction so many times in the few minutes allowed that the pilot was seriously thinking of turning the wireless receiver off. As it was, he found he was gradually descending closer to the ground and even worse, in the general direction of a solid looking hangar. He took the only action open to him in the interests of safety and landed. Speed far in excess of normal the aircraft bounced like a demented kangaroo and came to rest on its propeller with an expensive sounding crack. A very red-faced member of the public walked away from the microphone muttering to his spouse, ". . . but I didn't tell him to do that, dear!"

When Sqdn Ldr Donald Fleming arrived to take over the fighter squadron that August, he was disillusioned to find that some officers of experience had been posted away. He was further disillusioned when a signal arrived from the Air Ministry making his unit a part of the new advanced striking force; a force dictated by the reorganisation and expansion of the service. It was also disconcerting to realise, in the shape of things, that his days spent flying the wonderful Hawker Fury II were numbered. Two months later they were flown to Catterick in Yorkshire and handed over to No 41 squadron.

His reaction on seeing Hawker Demons at Catterick was quite inexpressible. More so when he was informed that they were now his! Fleming had flown Demons in Egypt and found them considerably slower than Italian bombers of that period.

When he reached the last machine in a preliminary inspection it was difficult for him to hide his feelings. The disappointment at losing his Furys had been a blow from which he was still smarting. He had insisted on inspecting the Demons and now he wished he hadn't! They were a sorry looking lot, sagging fabric, evidence of corrosion and oil patches everywhere. There was no comparison with his gleaming single-seaters standing just a few yards away looking like fine tempered blades in a medieval tournament. He had an urge to fly the Furys back to Hawkinge.

He turned to the Flight Engineering Officer, whose repartee had failed him at the third machine. He thought it prudent to remain silent for the remainder of the inspection.

"Do these actually fly?" Fleming enquired with obvious sarcasm.

"They are all fully operational, Sir," the Flight Engineer answered, but added, "we considered that if they were going into storage it would be a waste of effort to . . ."

"Storage! Storage!" Fleming interrupted. "Who said anything about storage?"

"I thought they were for your storage unit at Hawkinge," explained the Flight Engineer looking at papers he carried clipped to a board.

Growing impatient Fleming raised an arm as if presenting the Demons for public approval.

"We had a storage unit once — BUT — this miserable collection of antiquated machinery are now No 25 squadron . . . God help us!" Fleming exclaimed.

The Demons were flown to Hawkinge the next day and still carried the red flash insignia of their previous owners. The C.O. ordered a thorough inspection and, in the first returns, three Demons were grounded because of corroded longerons and it was four weeks before the remainder were passed fit.

Ten days later two Demons collided over Tilmanstone Colliery near Dover, but this had nothing to do with aircraft serviceability. It was, nevertheless, the first accident involving the two-seaters and Fleming was naturally furious. Pilot Officer Cave managed to bale out of his spinning

One of the few photographs of No 25 squadron's Demons. The aircraft shown is K4526 and flown by Flt Lt 'Pat' Burke. (Sqdn Ldr P. Burke, DFC)

machine but A.C.II Dale was not as lucky and was killed. The other machine only suffered slight damage and returned with both occupants showing signs of shock.

It had been a big disappointment to the squadron having two-seaters, let alone having them second-hand. The Demon was a further variant of the Hart and designated a fighter rather than a light bomber. It had been in service since 1933, and used the Rolls-Royce Kestrel V engine, with the standard production model reaching 206 mph. Those operating with the Hawkinge squadron were lucky to reach 185 mph flat out!

Fighter production had made heavy demands on the popular Kestrel engine and, when a new aircraft was envisaged to replace the Army Co-operation Audax an alternative power unit was specified. The twenty-four cylinder Napier Dagger engine, on trial since 1933, was finally chosen to power the new Hawker Hector biplane to be built by the Westland Aircraft Company at Yeovil under licence.

The Dagger engine was an unusual design with two air ducts sucking away one above the other below on opposite sides of the engine cowling with a novel 'fish-gill' arrangement to the rear. The bakelight distributor cap with its harness of 24 leads just behind the propeller boss was virtually inaccessible and often cracked under extreme heat conditions. Despite RAF expansion the Army Co-operation squadron flew their Hectors for the next two years, but they had little affection for them.

The Hawker Hector — K9741 — of No 2 (AC) squadron about to be taxied out onto the field with Flt Lt Andrew Geddes at the controls.   (Air Cdre A. J. W. Geddes, CBE, DSO)

Donald Fleming had many stories to tell of his time spent at Hawkinge but none were as strange to relate as this one.

At nearby Lympne aerodrome the Cinque Ports Flying Club had been in the habit of taking an early morning flight to Shoreham and back on Sundays. These 'dawn patrols' were a weekly event and they usually left early so that newcomers to the Club could practice their circuits and bumps afterwards.

The owner of a particularly fine B.A.Swallow light aeroplane had left it in charge of a young and delighted apprentice, whilst he returned to the Club Room for something or other. Quite unbeknown to the owner the apprentice thought it would save time if he started the engine. He checked petrol ON, switched on and went to the front end of the aeroplane to swing the little propeller. After several unsuccessful attempts he decided the carburettor might have flooded and so returned to the cockpit to switch OFF and set the throttle to WIDE OPEN. Back to the front end once again he swung the propeller anti-clockwise to clear the engine. Satisfied, he returned to the cockpit and switched ON but forgot the throttle setting. Back to the propeller he gave it an almighty swing and the little Cirrus engine coughed and roared into life.

Some ten minutes later, Fleming happened to be enjoying the solitude of his garden as service stations were usually as dead as the proverbial Do-Do at week ends, when the sound of a light aeroplane engine overhead gave some mild interest. He saw the Swallow just as it gave a pirouette then doubled back on its tracks and dived almost vertically towards the C.O.'s house. It then flicked over at a most unusual angle and carried out a series of dives but each time it did so it inexplicably veered off course and suddenly righted itself. Fleming took a note of the registration letters and dashed indoors to his phone.

"Hello — Hello — is that the Cinque Ports Flying Club, it is? — this is Squadron Leader Fleming here — C.O. of Hawkinge. I wish to speak to someone about one of your light aeroplanes — its making a damned nuisance over my house and, quite frankly this chap is going to do himself a mischief if he doesn't watch out — might even kill someone in the process too — what say? — yes its a white Swallow!"

Meanwhile at Lympne the apprentice was trying to give some kind of intelligent account of what actually happened to club officials. Evidently he had jumped clear when the engine had spluttered and started but was not quite quick enough and was bowled over by a wing-tip. The owner remembered the tail trim lever had been left well back from the previous landing. The little Swallow had gathered speed and actually took off leaving behind a very shaken apprentice. There followed a slow, rather flat climbing turn to the left up to about 500 feet and, with a stiff breeze from the West to help matters, the Swallow gradually drifted towards Folkestone.

The local Police and Fire Service were immediately alerted, for it seemed quite probable, taking all things into consideration, that the runaway might crash in the middle of the town with disastrous results. Club members got into their cars and led by a local constable on a motorcycle went off in pursuit.

Fleming had been told, "I'm afraid there isn't anyone in the aeroplane!"

He was not a little put out by this and bellowed down the receiver, "What! — I'm no fool, this chap who ever he is. . . .", the C.O. began, but was interrupted.

"I tell you Sir — there isn't anyone on board that aeroplane — it's flying by itself — in fact Sir — we are looking for it at this minute!"

"The Devil you are!", shouted the C.O., but before he could utter another word there was the sound of breaking wood intermingled with various other noises synonymous to a heavy landing of sorts. He slammed the receiver down and stormed outside. The runaway, probably affected by a down-draught, had attempted to land in a small field close by. It had been a neat three-point landing and had there been someone available to close the throttle it might have been a rough but reasonable arrival. As it was, the Swallow had careered across the field and finished up as a heap of matchwood. Its centre section with the two cockpits was, however, intact which speaks highly for the ruggedness of the wooden construction. Had there been a crew of two on board it is quite likely they would have got off with little more than a bad fright.

Fleming telephoned Lympne again, "It's crashed — the bloody fool has crashed — can't find the pilot anywhere!"

Back came the reply from Lympne, "I am the pilot!"

CHAPTER FIVE
The Awakening 1938–1939

Twenty years of peace had lulled the senses so that even the mere threat of war seemed unreal and incomprehensible to the British. But even so there was an uneasy feeling in 1938 which made the pessimists sit up and take notice. Incidents and situations boiled, refugees fleeing from the Continent brought stories of tragedy and despair. Here in England we were disturbed to find the Hendon display cancelled. This must have been a guide to the more astute that something of major importance was about to take place.

In March German troops had goose-stepped their way into Austria. Our own air staff were moved to even greater efforts with the RAF's expansion. New units were being formed and, by comparison with the well-equipped German Air Force, we could just about muster one hundred new monoplane fighters by the time Hitler broke his pledge. But that was in the following year.

In June 1938, the Supermarine Spitfire, the latest of our eight-gun monoplane fighters, began to fly operationally. It has been said that our factories were unable to make the quantities required had it been necessary through enemy action, and this could have been said for most of our armament factory production. Few people realised at the time that Hitler had decided to open up a full scale war in that year, against France and Great Britain, we would most likely have been rapidly defeated. It was fortunate for us that he gave our nation a year's grace.

Such rapid reorganisation, designed to produce a modern air arm capable of throwing back a powerful aggressor, hardly touched Hawinge at all. Some training programmes did accelerate and No 2 squadron was the first away to Aldergrove. In their absence No 25 squadron stepped up their night flying techniques until they left for Ireland in May.

Their flight to Ireland was not without incident. Fleming addressed his pilots in the briefing room the day before they were to leave.

"Gentlemen — we will fly to Catterick tomorrow in three flights of four aircraft, each flight will leave at half-hour intervals and will follow the same route, a route which will take you to Basingstoke — Oxford — Digby and finally Catterick. I will fly with 'C' Flight and hope to see you all at lunch!" He then gave the take-off times and informed them that the Flight Engineering Officer was confident that every machine was in 'tip-top' condition.

The meteorological report was a rather gloomy forecast and, because of it, Fleming advanced 'A' Flight's departure with subsequent advancements of the other two Flights. There was no problem getting the Flights off the next day but, because of heavy rain and thunder storms on route, the C.O. landed at Digby. He was confident of meeting the rest of the squadron there. They were not.

With the weather closing in fast and low cloud covering a considerable area of the British Isles, the intrepid C.O. took off with the rest of his Flight tucked in close like baby chicks around a mother hen. Visibility was atrocious whilst he followed a maze of railway lines criss-crossing every few miles. They eventually reached Catterick where the C.O. was told he was the only Flight to have landed. Fleming went off to lunch and, part way through his meal, he was interrupted by a waiter.

"Excuse me Sir — it seems there are Demons at rest in nearly every field in Yorkshire Sir."

Donald Fleming spent the remainder of the day locating his 'chicks' followed by a petrol bowser.

The air exercise for 1938 turned out to be one of adventure with over 900 aircraft taking part in one of the biggest peace-time shows of strength. It was a 'war-game' of mock battles and attacks ranging from the Thames to Lincoln, under the command of Air Marshal Sir Hugh Dowding.

For the five Auxillary squadrons using Hawkinge during that period the highlight must surely have been the occasion when No 602 (City of Glasgow) squadron went on a day trip to Boulogne, at the expense of their C.O. The airfield returned to a normal pace when the exercise had finished but No 25 had heard a rumour they were to re-equip with the Gloster Gladiator. That rumour became true when a signal was received to ferry their Demons to Hendon. Pilots were jubilant at the prospect of flying single-seaters, although they would have preferred one of the new monoplanes instead.

Low cloud rolled in obscuring the outlying hills on the day the Demons were to depart. One Flight had already got off before dense fog came down. Four machines stood at their take off point with propellers idling in swirling mists. It lifted slightly, just enough to get them on their way. Fleming watched them take off. The last machine, piloted by a New Zealander, Pilot Officer Bonar R. Walley, whose passenger was a university graduate, a Scot called Law, suddenly and for no apparent reason, turned right instead of left. Muffled sounds of a crashing aircraft was a macabre epitaph reminding everyone of that golden rule, 'turn left' — always turn left! Both occupants were killed outright.

Eleven camouflaged Gloster Gladiators were taken on charge from No 56 squadron and a further three arrived from No 65 squadron. The total was raised to nineteen when five more arrived from the Bristol factory. Nicknamed the 'Glad' it was an excellent fighter with very few vices, although night flying became rather more sedate and needed just that finer edge of expertise when recovering from a spin.

By a mere quirk of fate a piece of rag fouled the petrol feed dome of a No 2 squadron Hector, just two days before they were due to leave for Friday

Flt Lt Peter W. Stansfeld of No 2 (AC) squadron with his 'For Valour' star and ribbon presented by Station C.O.
(P. W. Stansfeld)

Wg Cmdr 'Bobby' George – Sqdn Ldr W. A. Opie – Flt Lt P. W. Stansfeld.
(P. W. Stansfeld)

Wood. Piloted by Wimbush the machine only managed to reach fifty feet before the engine stopped. Fixed to the cockpit floor by his 'dog-chain' the Observer-Gunner was the only casualty when the aircraft sank into soft earth and overturned.

Whilst at Friday Wood No 2 squadron received a signal informing them that they were to receive the new Westland Lysander. Deliveries were held back until they returned to Hawkinge and, of the sixty-six Lysanders built in the first batch, sixteen were delivered to the Hawkinge squadron. The honour of collecting the first one fell to Flt Lt Peter Stansfeld, who was greeted on his return by a battery of cameras. Wing Commander Bobby George, the station C.O., had laid on a reception committee and presented to Stansfeld a large six-pointed star inscribed 'For Valour' which was tied to a wide band of red ribbon.

Designed to replace the Audax and Hectors the Lysander, a single high-wing monoplane with fixed undercarriage was a fairly large aircraft which could operate from very small fields. Affectionately called the 'Lissie' it did some stirling work in the years ahead. Flt Lt Geddes brought the second

Blenheim 1F — L1440 — of No 25 squadron landing at Hawkinge 1938.   (Rex Puttee)

The Western Lysander L4698 photographed over Hawkinge with Flt Lt Andrew Geddes at the controls. This machine was the second to arrive from Yeovil.

(Air Cdre A. J. W. Geddes, CBE, DSO)

machine back to the aerodrome from Yeovil and he could not resist the temptation to stunt it. He threw the Lysander into a loop and did the usual slow roll off the top but noticed with some annoyance a slight fall-off in flying performance. It was found later to have been caused by a broken hinge which had snapped on the brake-slots. Because of that little escapade future aircraft were modified at the factory.

I do not suppose for one moment that the Hawkinge fighter squadron was any less ambitious or less proud of its background and capabilities than any other tip-top fighting unit in the Royal Air Force. But all the same a kind of gloom settled over the personnel like some monstrous cloud when, on 10th December, they watched a twin-engined Blenheim fighter-bomber make its début. Of course the odd typewritten signal had been observed with casual but calculated interest. Soon afterwards four new 12,000 gallon fuel tanks were installed.

Filling them was completed one Friday afternoon. A hastily convened Court of enquiry the following Monday failed to find the culprit who had left the controlling valves open. Remarkably no one had thrown a lighted match onto the flooded airfield!

The European crisis was now beginning to make itself felt at the aerodrome. All ranks had been recalled from leave a couple of months previously and gate passes were now necessary for anyone leaving camp. Buildings had received their first coat of camouflage of drab green and matt black, and glass windows had black cloth draped at their sides. Thousands of sandbags were stored in the Clerk of Works building.

Conversion training began in the new year and proved a lengthy process as Gladiators were still being flown in February. But in spite of a few vices the Blenheim was a pleasant machine to fly, although pilots never had that freedom of individuality enjoyed with the more manouvrable single-seaters.

Sqdn Ldr Donald Fleming, who was first commissioned at the age of seventeen and had served with the RFC, moved away to form a new fighter squadron in Scotland. His place was taken by Sqdn Ldr J. R. Halling-Pott who, within four months, had to sit on a board of enquiry over the loss of one Blenheim.

The artificial horizon on the Blenheim 1F worked from a Venturi tube and was subject to icing. On May 18th, Sgt Pilot J. G. Lindgard got into difficulties over Dartford on entering extemely turbulent storm clouds at 13,000 feet. The tube iced up and resulted in complete loss of control. Lindgard gave instructions to his crew to bale out and held on to the bucking machine down to 1,200 feet. With considerable difficulty owing to the gyrations of the aircraft, he jumped himself. Unbeknown to him, his navigator had not jumped, and perished in the crash.

Another crash ended in tragedy when No 2 squadron lost a Lysander. Display practice, a feature of flying for both the Hawkinge squadrons, always began a couple of weeks before the Empire Air Day was due.

Practice proves perfect they say, but Andrew Geddes looked on in horror as a Lysander, flown by Flt Lt Petrie, stalled and put a wing into the ground, killing himself and L. A. C. Stacey. This particular stunt, if it can be called that, was not difficult and required two aircraft to fly towards each other on a converging course one slightly above the other. It had been done on numerous occasions. Petrie was in the lower machine, its propeller in fine pitch and its nose well up doing about 60 mph at forty feet above ground level. The higher machine with Geddes at the controls was doing about 160 mph and had just reached the circle in the middle of the flying field when he saw Petrie's machine flounder and crash.

Vast crowds poured into the aerodrome open day a few weeks later, at least nine or ten thousand crammed the lanes and roads of the village. Lost children turned up in the most unlikely places. A mess steward discovered one youngster about to sample the wine rack. Another had to be rescued from the billowing folds of a tangled display parachute. The Fire Tender, left unattended briefly, was about to be started and put in gear when red-faced airmen jumped on the running board just in time.

The public little realised this would be their last opportunity to view the RAF at such close quarters. The dark shadows of the German war-machine were already rolling towards them bringing with it death, destruction, heartbreak and fear. Hawkinge displayed a strange mixture of weaponry and lambs, camouflaged aircraft and blossom. It was difficult to evaluate such a concoction. For years the Air Ministry had displayed critical stagnation in aircraft design policy and had produced a constant stream of biplane variants. There had seemed little regard for the future. We were still using ·303 amunition. One wondered if we had advanced at all. Of our monoplane fighters that the public had heard so much about, only one was displayed at the aerodrome, and that was kept behind a roped enclosure. The hangars were now huge forbidding structures, for the ornamental trees and shrubs had withered beneath the toxic camouflage paintwork. One could sense the gloom which hung in the air in thick folds, almost suffocating in its intensity.

Whilst No 25 Squadron were away at Sutton Bridge, completing their training programme they were posted to RAF Northolt. The reason given was that the Blenheim required hard-based runways from which to operate, not slippery grass fields. Whatever the reason it gave another sinister twist to the aerodrome's future. It had been the home of that famous fighter squadron for nineteen years. Now there began a colder, harsher era in the aerodrome's history. Looking back to those peaceful years it had been for most a great flying adventure. But young men eager for excitement were now to find a more serious fulfilment to their dreams. Had they absorbed the knowledge imparted by their instructors? If they had, then they were all confident men. But even confident men, flying unfamiliar patterns in a hostile sky, would find it difficult to survive the terrors of warfare.

CHAPTER SIX
The Storm Begins, September 1939–May 1940

Inevitably full mobilisation of the three Services was the natural outcome when Great Britain declared war on Germany on 3rd September 1939.

Not so obvious and seen by many as a retrograde step, was that RAF Hawkinge was to become No 3 Recruit Training Pool. No one from the Station C.O. down could understand how a front-line fighter station of vital importance now that war was declared, could possibly be anything else other than a fighter station. But even so, over three hundred raw recruits arrived for their initial training in torrential rain, flooding and a sea of mud.

No 2 (AC) squadron received a signal to move to France within twenty-four hours. Equipment went by road and ship and the Lysanders flew to Drucat and Abbeville a week later. Army Officers arrived to discuss airfield defences and with them came two from Military Intelligence to investigate rumours of an illegal transmitter reported in the vicinity.

The first German aircraft was reported in the area on 20th November, flying at about 3,000 feet. The Dover anti-aircraft guns fired a few rounds but no air raid warning had been given. 'E' Company 6th Buffs Regiment were manning light machine guns placed at strategic sites around the aerodrome boundary. No one had as yet decided whether light anti-aircraft guns should be installed.

A decision had been made to re-camouflage the whole airfield. It had already been camouflaged around the time of the Munich crisis when the Gladiators had also lost their silver glory. Now every building, post, road and path, even the grass was sprayed in kaleidoscopic greens, browns and deep yellows. From the air the airfield resembled a patchwork quilt. No one had considered the village. It stood out in complete contrast. Sheep, who had been used to crop the grass were given to fits of sneezing when the toxic paint carried towards them. The Clerk of Works never did find the culprit who sprayed his car! Serious preparations for some kind of airfield defence resulted in thousands of earth-fiilled sandbags being placed round doors, windows and hastily dug slit-trenches. Dozens of gas-detector posts were struck in the ground, an event which brought a shudder to those old enough to remember the previous war.

In the third week of December a completely new sound broke the morning stillness when the Hawker Hurricanes of No 3 squadron vied for positions in circuit to make their landings. Because of the newly camouflaged field Sqdn Ldr Gifford was unsure where the airfield boundary began.

Lympne aerodrome stood some five miles to the West and had become HMS Buzzard overnight. It was soon teeming with Navy personnel who, for some obscure reasoning, were brought over to Hawkinge to be taught aircraft identifiction! Perhaps it was to combine the exercise with one of Jack Buchanan's stage shows playing in the gymnasium.

The traditional White Christmas of 1939 passed quietly. It was a strange and somewhat unusual Christmas for the local inhabitants because the aerodrome seemed to have completely discarded its peacetime associations. A transformation had taken place. Airmen, strangers to each other listened to the news broadcasts which somehow implied feelings of involvement with the suffering thousands fleeing from the Continent. Pilots apprehensively contemplated the future. No one really felt in festive mood by New Year's Eve. The situation looked bleak and the future most unpredictable. But then, there was also an uncanny air of excitement, as Hurricanes patrolled the coastline daily.

During the daylight hours retired gentlemen of the village and surrounding districts sat on Windsor chairs at strategic points around the aerodrome perimeter and in the most exposed positions imaginable. As members of the Local Defence Volunteers, they clutched ancient Short Lee-Enfield rifles recently brought out of mothballs and, although mechanically useless without ammunition, they seemed to symbolise our nation's capacity for the bizarre.

The second heavy snowfall of the winter engulfed the area in the last two weeks of January. With tractor, snow-plough and shovels, airmen cleared a sufficient area of the field to enable No 3 squadron Hurricanes to leave for Kenley. What they didn't expect was three Blenheims of No 500 squadron to make use of their labours during a snow storm. The Blenheims had got themselves lost and had been flying around for some considerable time before they found Hawkinge. Under dark heavy skies airmen toiled non-stop to free the aerodrome of this white blanket which had formed almost impossible barriers. Disillusioned 'erks' found the task intolerable and made igloos and snowmen, the former as refuge from prying eyes but the latter bore a remarkable likeness to the Warrant Officer!

No 16 squadron, another Army Co-operation unit and the last of its kind to remain this side of the English Channel, moved to Hawkinge with their eighteen Lysanders where they began to train in field support duties. Their posting seemed to coincide with Hawkinge being re-allocated to Fighter Command, and a convoy of Queen Marys which arrived from RAF Henlow with dismembered aircraft and equipment belonging to No 1 Pilotless Aircraft Unit. It was an impressive array of bits and pieces unloaded into a hangar where airmen poked and prodded, lifted sheeting and discussed its usefulness. Mechanics and riggers were however, disillusioned when they learned that these prized possessions, now totalling twenty-six Tiger Moths and one or two Queen Bees were to remain crated.

'E' Company of the 6th Buffs Regiment on defence duties at RAF Hawkinge 1940. This photograph was taken outside the Reindene House H.Q. in Reindene Wood.

(Ron Cook)

But a couple of Boffins arrived the following month from the RAE at Farnborough and set about erecting tall lattice pylons connected by wires to an enormous wireless cabinet. Soon afterwards a Queen Bee pilotless aircraft began flying around the Folkestone area at varying heights and speeds operated by a complex box of trickery. Pat Osbourne, one of the Boffins remembers:

"It was at the time when unarmed Tiger moths and privately owned light aeroplanes, pressed into war service, were flying up and down the English Channel in a strategic bid to out-fox Goering into believing we had more aircraft than we really had. Whether we, at Hawkinge, with our radio equipment and pilotless aircraft added to Goering's confusion we will probably never know! — but it was fun all the same."

Lysanders, pilotless aircraft and an Autogyro piloted by a Dr Tingey who was busily re-calibrating the Dover Radar system, proved too much for the Recruiting Training Pool who promptly left.

Also in February a Flg Off Scott-Farnie began to organise a listening post at the aerodrome in a disused building. Long before hostilities had began Great Britain, like other countries, had operated long-range monitoring of foreign radio broadcasts which became the forerunner of radio intelligence. It was not then highly technical or terribly well organised, but even before the fall of France, listening to German transmissions proved most valuable.

To operate the short-wave receivers translators were needed and eventually German speaking WAAFs were found who were to maintain a twenty-four watch. These girls, specially selected and immediately promoted to the rank of sergeant moved from their original cramped conditions to Maypole Cottage, a secluded house near the village. The girls were to provide a valuable service by working very long hours recording complicated messages by primitive longhand methods. Once firmly established the wireless unit became instrumental in discovering frequencies used by German 'E' Boats. In a very short space of time similar wireless posts were set up around the English coasts.

A Sqdn Ldr Eayrs arrived one day in March with a piece of paper stuffed in a pocket which gave him permission to form another Army Co-operation squadron. It was to be numbered 416 and, soon after his arrival, some ancient Lysanders began to arrive from St Athen, S. Wales. Everything about the unit seemed vague. Airmen borrowed tools and bits and pieces to complete some tasks only to learn that the unit would be disbanded on 1st April! They wondered if it was the traditional April-Fools joke. On 19th of the month it reformed again!.

During an affiliation exercise with No 16 squadron Lysanders, a Hurricane of No 3 squadron, piloted by Sgt Lomay, spun out of control and dived to the ground just outside the aerodrome boundary. It was the first fatality to occur at the aerodrome since hostilities had begun. Within a week No 16 squadron left for France.

The Commanding Officer of Biggin Hill Sector Station flew down one day to inspect the building of dispersal pens. Three were located next to Killing Wood and another three were near Gibraltar Lane.

The glorious month of May, when spring blossom turns the Kentish fruit fields into carpets of pink and white, brought with it chaos and uncertainty to our troops in France. As a back-up to their efforts enemy positions, rapidly changing minute by minute, were attacked time and again by our Blenheim medium bombers with fighter escort. Although Hawkinge had been found unsuitable from which to operate these particular aircraft, it was now a matter of urgency to provide a jump-off for these low-level attacks. Both Nos 25 and 604 squadrons participated in these sorties and used the aerodrome facilities.

As the French and British armies were being pushed back towards the Channel coast a mammoth evacuation programme was prepared under the code name of 'Dynamo' and commanded by Vice-Admiral Ramsey at Dover. Hawkinge became an important part of this operation when an HQ called 'Back Component' was set up there. It was under the command of Air Vice-Marshal C. H. B. Blount, whose task was not to be envied. He was expected to collate evidence to assist with evacuating thousands of troops along an area of coast which, hourly, diminished in size as defensive positions were overrun. Information was extremely scarce due to inadequate wireless equipment. He relied therefore, on reports given by returning aircrew supplemented with information gleaned from radio messages intercepted by the girls in the experimental wireless section.

As the evacuation progressed the aerodrome became over-crowded with aircraft of all types arriving from the fighting areas and many showing signs of combat damage and fatigue. The majority were quickly refuelled and dispersed to inland aerodromes while others, obviously too dangerous to fly were wheeled into one of the hangars. There was one Lysander, attacked by Bf 109s over Boulogne, which had sustained a terrific pounding but still managed to make Hawkinge. The pilot, Plt Off Scotter, was amazed to find the undercarriage, fuel-tank and wings hanging by the merest thread of metal!

The AOC No 11 Group, Air Vice-Marshal Keith Park, visited the beaches at Dunkirk in his Hurricane and remained at Hawkinge for a considerable time afterwards advising and organiing the air cover. Before he left he witnessed the arrival of just a handful of Lysanders, the only survivors of No 613 (AC) squadron. The original composite force of sixteen aircraft had come under tremendous ground fire whilst dropping supplies and dive-bombing enemy troop positions. Some of the aircraft were blown clean out of the sky. Crews perished without any chance of survival.

No 2 squadron, like others, also suffered severe casualties both in aircraft and personnel. Just before Dunkirk they operated deep into France, single machines at ten-minute intervals without fighter cover. In answer to urgent calls for assistance on 26th May, eight Lysanders of the squadron took off from Hawkinge to drop supplies to those defending Calais. Whilst metal containers filled with water, food and ammunition were being dropped from as low as fifty feet, they were subjected to murderous ground fire. Two aircraft were brought down in as many minutes and every aircraft was damaged. The shortage of Lysanders became acute, so much so that later dropping sorties over the same area included obsolete Hector biplanes!

The mode of attack, although gallant in every respect, proved useless in stopping the advancing German Panzer Divisions.

Despite these enormous odds the AC crews flew sortie after sortie into dense anti-aircraft fire. On one occasion no less than 48 canisters were dropped on the garrison below and only one fell outside the parade ground.

Standing fighter patrols were operated over the beaches almost continuously on a front extending some ten miles. Using Hawkinge throughout the withdrawal operation were the Spitfires of No 41 squadron, the Hurricanes of No 245 squadron and No 605 squadron who lost their C.O. Sqdn Ldr Perry. The Luftwaffe were now able to use captured Belgian and French airfields and therefore were operating from a considerably shorter range, often making their attacks upon columns of troops immediately our patrolling fighters had returned to refuel and rearm.

There was a build up of enemy activity after the Dunkirk evacuation. As a front-line satellite airfield Hawkinge was now to be used continuously for rearming and refuelling fighter aircraft. The personnel of No 11 Servicing Flight were to set up a remarkable record of thoroughness and efficiency whilst dealing with the needs of countless fighters which dropped in without warning or ceremony before, during and after combat. Aircraft landed with petrol tanks reading empty, hydraulics shot away, ammunition expended, engines alight, control surfaces crumpled and trailing torn fabric like bunting. Some of the hasty landings would have made the hair of any instructor stand on end. Aircraft clipped the perimeter trees and hedges, ploughed through fences and dug deep furrows in the turf. Machines stood up on their propellers, some cartwheeled to destruction, while others skidded across the field on their cockpits. Even a pirouette was not uncommon.

The victories won by pilots in the air would never have been achieved without the conscientious efforts of the ground crews. Sometimes their cheerfulness dispelled the fears of young pilots. Damaged aircraft were repaired and patched with speed. Injured pilots were removed carefully from their twisted cockpits while vomit and blood were washed from the floors.

No 610 (County of Chester) squadron Spitfires refuelling at Hawkinge, July 1940.

(Fox Photos Ltd)

CHAPTER SEVEN

Blue Skys and Scrambles June 1940 — July, 1940

Now that France had fallen the Battle of Britain was to begin.

The first week in July brought No 1 squadron Hurricanes down to Hawkinge to take up the defensive role now envisaged. One flight of aircraft were sent on alternate days.

Following the advice of many Army Officers, including that of Brigadier Roupel, VC, airfield defences had, by and large, taken on some semblance of order. Trenches and dugouts were established but incredibly, although 3″ anti-aircraft guns had been mentioned, there was no provision made to instal heavy calibre guns. The anti-aircraft units were at the same time under the direction of Fighter Command, and Air Vice-Marshal Dowding was forced to move the majority of heavy guns to positions around the industrial towns and cities with London a priority.

The airfield was not well defended. By the end of May, four 40 mm Bofors units had been sited more or less on static sites, within the airfield perimeter. There were of course the official complement of eight .303 machine guns which had always been allocated to airfields. However, on 11th June, it had been reported that there was a shortage of Lewis ammunition drums. The same report suggested that each machine gun was to have, at the minimum, six 97-round drums per gun. It also recommended that army detachments were to have at least 50 rounds of ammunition for each rifle. Four 20 mm Hispano cannons were also sited and one Oerlikon, which somehow had been salvaged from a sunken ship off Dover. Beyond the airfield other Bofors units, completely mobile with crews living under canvas, were sited strategically. A couple of three-ton lorries mounted a Bren-gun from the scarfe opening in the cab roof and one lorry in particular at Hawkinge, called the Armadillo, was armoured with quarter-inch steel plate.

A further report, dated 22nd June, thought the camouflage on buildings was rather faint and that it should be renewed. Seventeen aircraft were seen on the aerodrome on that occasion and the reporting officer was quite satisfied with their dispersal. He mentioned one conspicuously painted Tiger Moth, standing beside a hangar and thought the yellow coloured machine served to demonstrate the advantage of camouflage. The Inspector General's report about a month later suggested the use of 'Dummy' aircraft in the new dispersal pens and putting the real aircraft under trees. The report further stated that the 'Dummy aircraft' would provide a conspicuous target which enemy aircraft would be induced to attack!

Towards the end of June the experimental rockets called Parachute and Cable (PAC) were installed. This bizarre invention was used to supplement the deficiencies of airfield defence. The rockets, based on the Schurmully marine sevice were fired from a tube-like contraption resembling a length of guttering about four feet long attached to a swivel base plate. They were set off in batches of eight by a four volt battery. Coiled in a box near the base were long lengths of piano wire attached to each rocket. Theoretically, the rocket projectile would reach a height of about 600 feet trailing the wire behind it. A sudden jerk of the wire released a small parachute which suspended the wire in the path of an enemy aircraft.

This well meaning device was unsuccessful when operated at Hawkinge, although a claim was made a year later during a tip-and-run raid. But the first trials of the PAC equipment (whether fired by accident or design has never been established) resulted in a hilarious shambles. The 3'' projectiles flew up into the sky in all directions each crossing the path of another allowing the wires to become hopelessly entangled. The combined weight of the enmeshed wire proved too much for the little parachutes which sank to earth before the rockets had given off their best. They littered the airfield fizzing and burning like giant squibs at a Guy Fawkes gala night.

By this time of course a threat of invasion was in the offing. No one knew for certain if Hitler intended to invade the British Isles or not. The threat was enough to encourage the authorities to stick wooden poles in fields to combat expected glider landings. Road blocks were set up on either side of the village of Hawkinge and rolls of barbed wire were strewn about the countryside with artful angenuity. Signposts disappeared overnight. All the main approach roads, buildings and important installations were mined with eight feet lengths of drainpipe which, wired together in batches of six, were to be fired from a central point.

When the German armed forces stood along the Channel coast looking across at Kent and Sussex, now within easy reach of their aircraft, our defence on the ground was hardly a powerful force to throw against the victorious German Panzer Divisions now poised to strike in our direction.

It was about then that the War Cabinet heard these words from the Chief of Staff; "Should the enemy succeed in establishing a force, with its vehicles, firmly ashore, the Army in the United Kingdom, which is very short of equipment, has not got the offensive power to drive it out . . . the crux of the matter is air superiority."

On June 18th, Winston Churchill had said, " . . . I expect the Battle of Britain to begin." I'm sure he never invisaged the aerial battles fought with such intensity by our young fighter pilots to whom he later referred to saying, " . . . This was their finest hour."

In just a few weeks German armed forces had conquered Norway, Denmark, Belgium, Holland and France. Now it was our turn to feel the weight of Goering's Luftwaffe, at the time reputed to be the strongest air force in the world. The preliminary air attacks, the prelude to Alder Tag (Eagle Day), opened up on Channel convoys, a pattern which lasted a month.

Pilots of No 32 squadron relax between sorties at Hawkinge during the Battle of Britain. Left to right:—Plt Off R. P. Smythe – Plt Off J. E. Proctor – Plt Off M. R. Gillman – Flt Lt P. M. Brothers – Plt Off D. H. Grice – Plt Off P. M. Gardner – Plt Off A. E. Eckford.

(Fox Photos Ltd.)

We began to concentrate on German barges now lying in French harbours. HRH King George VI watched a formation of Blenheims circle the aerodrome on 1st July, waiting for their Spitfire escort.

Throughout July the daily flying hours gradually increased with as many as five and sometimes seven 'scrambles' to intercept raiders penetrating our air space. Squadrons on 'advanced readiness' arrived at Hawkinge on a day-to-day basis and included No 501, 32, 72, 64 and 610. No 79 squadron Hurricanes flew down in the first week of July, becoming involved in pitched battles against considerable odds. Another, No 245 squadron, had fifteen Hurricanes available on 1st July, but within three weeks were moved away from the fighting zone because of low strength.

Hitler's invasion plan for South East England demanded air superiority and with it, the complete destruction of Fighter Command. In consequence the German air force supreme command issued orders on 2nd July in respect of their air onslaught against Britain.

It was as a result of one of these bomber group interceptions that Plt Off K. R. Gillman, flying a Hurricane of No 32 squadron, force landed at the airfield one evening. The attack by a force of Do 17s on 4th July was concentrated on a convoy just East of Dover. No 79 squadron had scrambled eight available Hurricanes at about two o'clock and within minutes had lost sight of Sgt H. Cartright who was last seen crashing into the sea off St Margaret's Bay. No 32 squadron were also involved and Plt Off R. F. Smythe managed to shoot down two Bf 109 fighters near Folkestone.

A heavily damaged Spitfire piloted by Sub Lt F. Dawson-Paul, attached to No 64 squadron from the Fleet Air Arm, bounced so hard on landing that both oleo legs collapsed. Earlier that day a Heinkel 111 of 8 Staffel KG1 ploughed into the sea off Lydden Spout near Dover. The crew of five swam ashore and were picked up by an anti-aircraft gun crew who conveyed them to Hawkinge. Locked in the guardroom at the main gate they became VIPs as many airmen thought up excuses to take a look at the enemy at close quarters.

At 2.30 pm on Sunday 7th July, a large convoy was under attack off Dover. Over 40 DO 17s of KGII were milling around the sky like a swarm of wasps. No 79 squadron was scrambled from the airfield and their C.O., Sqdn Ldr J. D. C. Joslin, last to leave the grass, was seen climbing steeply to catch the remainder of his squadron. He never reached them. On the outskirts of Dover his Hurricane caught the full blast of a Messerschmitt who had pounced from out of the sun. Joslin died in the cockpit when his aircraft crashed near Chilverton Elms. On the following day yet another convoy was being attacked in the Straits. No 79 squadron had already suffered heavy losses and was to lose two more on this day. Nine Hurricanes scrambled and were soon bounced while they were still climbing. Plt Off J. E. R. Wood was the first casualty. His Hurricane went down in flames and his body was later recovered from the sea by naval launch. Flg Off R. F. Smythe of No 32 squadron brought his crippled Hurricane back with the engine alight. The second casualty of No 79 squadron was Flg Off E. W. Mitchell, whose Hurricane crashed at Temple Ewell near Dover.

By this time No 79 squadron was in need of a rest and was subsequently sent out of the fighting on 10th July. They had only just left the airfield when Sgt R. Carnall, flying a Hurricane of No 111 squadron, dropped onto the turf in a near dive putting the propeller into the ground. Three days later Sgt A. E. Binman of No 64 squadron, hit a number of times by anti-aircraft shells near Dover, wrestled with his Spitfire and managed to achieve a wheels-up landing in a nearby field.

As the air fighting increased more squadrons were thrown in to stem the flow of German infiltration. High octane fuel was in great demand. Thousands of rounds of ·303 amunition were now stored in No 3 hangar. Long hours spent at dispersals coupled with high flying, altitudes of 28,000 feet were not uncommon, with crash landings and parachute descents thrown in for good measure, all took their toll upon the young pilots. Nerves as taut as drumskins they became aged and tired. Some fell asleep in their cockpits between scrambles. Frayed nerves and lack of sleep were often the causes of landing approach accidents. Belly landings were all too frequent and misjudgment of height produced serious damage to valuable aircraft.

Pilots were expected to be on 'stand by' from as early as 5.00 am. One squadron in particular arrived at Hawkinge at 4.20 am. Aircraft were usually arranged in a rather haphazard way to minimise the possibility of attack damage, although the machines were still accessible for the inevitable scramble. Parachutes were usually left on top of the wing root, close to the cockpit with the straps hanging downwards in front of the leading edge. That way pilots were able to grasp the two shoulder straps and pull the body of the parachute from the wing as they moved towards the cockpit. Speed was essential, which is why the helmet with earphones already plugged into the socket, was usually left hanging over the reflector sight, just behind the windshield, or on top of the control column. By the time the pilot was seated in his cockpit he could start the engine almost immediately. So as not to exhaust the aircraft's own electrical system a mobile starter was connected to the engine to provide the additional power.

Each dispersal area was a self-contained community which comprised the ground crews, Riggers, Mechanics, Armourers, Wireless mechanics and the petrol bowser crew. Bell-tents provided additional accommodation to the wooden dispersal huts, around which were chairs used by the pilots. Aircraft recognition posters covered most of the interiors in the huts and the few remaining spaces were taken up with the inevitable pin-ups.

Fighter squadrons detached to Hawkinge took their turn with other units to maintain standing patrols in addition to scrambles and convoy protection sorties. Sometimes local anti-aircraft gun co-operation duties were also required. Occasionally, at squadron strength, they would hurtle across the Channel for a reconnaissance patrol to places like Amiens, Abbeville, Poix, Dieppe or Le Treport. By late evening as the red sun gave a warm glow to the sky, they would prepare to move back to their home base. Tired out they would take off singly or in pairs, some with canopies open while others had not bothered to don their flying helmets. The Spitfires or Hurricanes would rise above the village roof tops to turn, then disappear into the red sky until the next day.

The following day was often a mirror-image of the previous day. The 'waiting game' some called it. They were waiting for that shrill telephone bell to jangle on already taut nerves. Occasionally, after the order to scramble had been given, a counter order to 'stand by' would be received. This was often the case when enemy aircraft were hurtling back from their targets making for the coast. There our pilots would sit, strapped in their cockpits. The seconds would tick by. All eyes were watching the Flying Operations Room for that flash of colour which indicated a scramble. Above them they could see the vapour trails hanging like paper streamers through the haze. Then perhaps — at last, a Very Light would shoot into the air, hovering and spluttering above the windsock. Starter buttons were being pushed before the Very Light cartridge had fallen to the ground. Propellers would begin to turn, slowly at first, then the engine would fire causing puffs of blue smoke to appear at the exhaust stubbs. One after another of the Merlins would roar into life. Within seconds the starter battery cables would be pulled from their housing. Individually the aircraft would move forwards across the grass, tail wheels jigging as they hit tufts of grass. One by one the aircraft would form up into a swallow 'V' formation on the ground then, with a signal from the leader, there would be a gradual deepening note from the engines and the whole body of aircraft would move as one. After about one hundred yards or so the tail wheels would leave the ground and, gathering speed the machines would rise towards the perimeter.

Every aerodrome had its tragedies and, amongst those associated with RAF Hawkinge, probably that which involved No 141 squadron was one of the most poignant. They had flown down to this front-line airfield in the early hours of Friday 19th July, with their immaculate and gleaming Boulton Paul Defiants. The week before whilst at West Malling, the Defiants had each had fitted the new constant speed propeller, the three-bladed device which increased speed performance. It is sad to reflect that the deficiencies in firepower and manoeuvrability were not considered at the same time. The Defiant, however, was a comparatively new fighter for which the RAF held high hopes. It was a slim Merlin-powered monoplane with a crew of two, pilot and gunner but, unlike the Hurricane and Spitfire, carried no forward firing armament in its wings. Instead it was armed with a four-gun, manually-operated turret situated midway along the fuselage just aft of the cockpit.

Only two squadrons, No 141 and 264, had originally been equipped with this new fighter. The latter unit was reputed to have scored a success over the Dunkirk beaches by shooting down 37 enemy aircraft on just two sorties. Although that score has since been disputed since the absence of forward firing machine guns operated by the pilot was to prove disastrous in all subsequent air combats. No 141 squadron came close to being completely annihilated.

Unlike its twin No 141 did not shoot in anger until that fateful 19th July. Lunch on this Friday was interrupted by the wail of Folkestone sirens at 12.10 pm. By 12.18 the Luftwaffe were dropping bombs in and around Dover harbour. At 12.30 No 141 took off, although only nine out of the twelve Defiants managed to leave the airfield. Two developed engine faults and would not start, whilst the third could not complete its take off run. In three sections of three, line astern, the nine Defiants set course for Dungeness where they were further vectored to a point some ten miles North of Cap Gris Nez.

It was Flt Lt Lounden who first gave warning of about twenty or so Bf 109s diving at them from out of the sun. The perfectly formated Defiants opened out to bring their guns to bear on the targets. But the pilots of II/JG2, the famous Richtofen Geschwader, outmanoeuvred them. The most vulnerable part of the Defiant was the underside. The leader of the Messerschmitts dived below the British formation then screamed upwards until they were hanging on their propellers allowing each German pilot to select a target to fire at.

Almost immediately two Defiants broke away in flames and plummeted to the sea below. Plt Off J. R. Kemp, his gunner Sgt R. Crombie, Plt Off A. Howley and Sgt A. G. Curley, were unable to bail out. The remaining seven jockeyed for position like wired puppets in a desperate attempt to give their gunners some sort of advantage. Flashing aircraft were now tumbling over onto their backs below the Defiants. Sgt Powell was the first to send a Messerschmitt down in flames from the seething mass of spiralling machines from which ammunition cases and other debris was shed while they banked, spun and roared their way around the sky.

All the Defiants had been hit in the first attack. Plt Off I. N. McDougall wrestled with the controls of his machine after it had flipped over onto its back and dived for the sea. Traces of white Glycol from a punctured tank splattered against his windshield. He ordered his gunner Sgt J. F. Wise, to bail out, an almost impossible task in a Defiant. The turret was one of the most escape-proof contraptions ever devised. But Sgt Wise did manage the impossible and cleared the spinning aircraft. McDougall was ready to follow when the engine gave a cough and roared back into life. Battling with a machine reluctant to fly, he brought it back to Hawkinge and made some sort of landing. Sgt Wise, however, was never seen again. Flt Lt Lounden watched two more Defiants burst into flames and spin for the sea when he suddenly found himself the target of about a dozen Messerschmitts. Caught between murderous crossfire, he put the nose of his machine down in a frantic attempt to increase speed. Gaping holes appeared in the wings and the fuselage then flames and smoke gushed from the engine compartment. Lounden shouted through his microphone to Plt Off Farnes to bale out. He managed to nurse the stricken Defiant back towards the coast and only just made a field next to the village. The exhausted Plt Off Farnes was later picked up by the Ramsgate Lifeboat.

One Defiant with a 'Cock o' the North' motif painted on its engine cowling, ablaze from stem to stern, skimmed the waves in a desperate attempt to reach Hawkinge. Unable to regain height, the Rhodesian born pilot, Flt Lt I. D. G. Donald, struggled with his blazing aircraft as it streaked across Dover to enter the Elms Vale Valley. It flew into the side of a hill just four miles from Hawkinge killing the pilot and his gunner, Plt Off A. C. Hamilton.

Commanded by Sqdn Ldr J. Thompson, No 111 squadron had also been at Hawkinge early that morning, and had remained on 'stand by' since the Defiants had left. They were, however, scrambled in time to reach the decimated 'Cock Squadron' before all were slaughtered. Plt Off Simpson managed to shoot down one Bf 109 before the rest of them fled towards the French coast. Of the nine Defiants scrambled from the airfield only four got back, and of those, two were so badly shot up they were written off squadron strength almost immediately.

The first combat of No 141 squadron had ended in tragedy with seven Defiants lost, four pilots and six gunners killed. What was left, aircraft and crew, moved to Biggin Hill soon afterwards where survivors of the unit were released from further action.

But the action at Hawkinge was not yet over for the day. Sqdn Ldr Worrall, leading No 32 squadron had been scrambled from Hawkinge that afternoon. He took his Hurricanes through the Dover gun barrage to intercept Bf 109s which seemed to be everywhere. Flt Sgt Turner spotted a lone Bf 109 above the village of Whitfield. He went in to attack although he knew the Hurricane was no match for the German aircraft. He fired and then lost site of his quarry. The next thing that happened was seeing cannon shells blowing bits from his engine cowling. At little more than 2,000 feet Sgt Turner baled out after struggling to get the aircraft to steer away from the built-up areas of Dover. Dangling from his parachute he saw his Hurricane dive into a field of corn near the village of Church Hougham. Minutes later he struck the hard ashphalt surface of Folkestone Road, Dover.

There was no let-up in the Luftwaffe attacks during July. Our fighter defences relied upon the Hurricanes and Spitfires which daily enacted a kind of symbolic drama on a stage enveloping the whole of South East England. But catching the enemy at their maximum height always proved difficult. It was much easier to seek out individual bombers returning to the coast than to intercept by means of a long climb in the initial stages of a raid. Scrambles from a coastal airfield were often given too late to be effective. A climbing attack most often resulted in being bounced by German fighters.

The Hurricane bore the brunt of attacks in the early stages but, as Dowding later revealed, the average speed of the production Hurricane was only about 305 mph. This was far too slow when engaging enemy fighters but was ideal for tackling the bombers. Despite its inferior speed performance the Hurricane, due in part to its remarkable manoeuvrability, proved capable of holding its own. It was also very ruggedly constructed. A New Zealand pilot, Flt Lt Gibson of No 501 squadron, had cause to remember that outstanding feature when his own particular Hurricane burst into flames over Folkestone. Realising the blazing machine would be a danger to life and property he steered out to sea before bailing out. Sqdn Ldr Worrall leading Green section of No 32 squadron also had a similar experience whilst attacking Bf 109s over a convoy off Dover. With ammunition exhausted he broke for home. His engine was alight and he was too low to bale out successfully. With a dead engine just one mile from the airfield he gouged a huge furrow in a field. He ran from his hissing wreck as it burst into flames and exploded.

The sleek Spitfire was by no means a poor cousin to the Hurricane. On the contrary, it was faster and more sensitive and at certain heights, was able to outmanoeuvre the Bf 109. But one major defect on the early marks was the gravity-fed carburettor which caused fuel starvation when the aircraft was at a certain angle of incidence. A light aeroplane by comparison it was nonetheless able to sustain punishment like the Hurricane.

It seems incredulous that some pilots were able to nurse stricken aircraft for miles, playing for time, while they used every trick in the book to survive. One such incident comes to mind involving Flt Lt Gilbert of No 64 squadron, whose Spitfire had received a terrific pounding over Dover harbour. The radiator had been holed and glycol steam entered the cockpit. Large holes were torn in the wings and tail section. Amidst bullets from his adversary and shells from the Dover guns which followed his slow progress, Gilbert unfastened his harness, raised himself into the most precarious position with the canopy opened, and brought the crippled Spitfire back to Hawkinge.

There were so many wrecked aircraft laying around the aerodrome at this time the Engineering Officer was able to cannibalise to keep aircraft serviceable. Dowding was becoming concerned with the appalling fighter losses not only due to combat but due also to accidents. As a result he issued orders that a Flying Officer Discipline should be attached to each forward airfield to advise on aircraft handling. Further instructions outlined that pilots, some were barely twenty years of age, were to receive regular physical exercise and be given at least eight hours free time from duty. Few, if any, were given the opportunity unless they were wounded. Dowding's stern facial features earned him the name of 'stuffy' but beneath this veneer lay immense insight into the problems facing Fighter Command. His inspired leadership provided the necessary driving force, advising and chastising his squadron leaders but all the while appreciative of their feelings and unflinching loyalty. He became known as the 'father of the few' in much the same way as Lord Trenchard had been known as the 'father of the Royal Air Force'. Dowding spoke of the pilots as 'his boys'.

Just before lunch on 24th July, the Spitfires of No 610 squadron were approaching the airfield. An identity flare in the colour of the day fizzled to the ground. It was a timely gesture for although their arrival was known the sound of aircraft often induced the gunners to fire first and ask questions afterwards!

Light rain had been falling for the past hour with low cloud sweeping in over the airfield from the West. The Luftwaffe had been active over the Thames Estuary since early morning with a convoy as target. Another target presented itself in the Dover Straits which became the centre of attraction. The squadron scrambled just after lunch. The rain had stopped and there were blue patches of sky to be seen as the Spitfires, led by Sqdn Ldr Smith, climbed away from the village. Of the 560 sorties flown by the RAF that day only three of our aircraft were lost. Sadly one of them was Sqdn Ldr Smith.

During the fierce dog-fights over the Channel Smith's Spitfire received heavy damage but, as others had tried before, he steered his crippled aircraft towards Hawkinge. Airmen and civilians stopped their labours to watch the aircraft limping closer to the airfield boundary, losing height, its flaps fully extended and the undercarriage locked down. It suddenly altered course towards the cemetary, as if the pilot might have been wounded, but then righted itself and veered round nose down towards the airfield again. It was very low — too low. The undercarriage caught in tangled loops of barbed wire placed between the M.T. shed and the perimeter fence. The Spitfire swung round in a half circle and smashed with sickening force against the brickwork. Running airmen stopped in their tracks as ammunition exploded from the wing guns. Flames enveloped the wrecked aircraft. It was impossible to reach the cockpit. Sqdn Ldr Smith had been killed.

Out of ammunition and low on fuel the remainder of the squadron returned to see the smouldering wreckage below them. When they learned of their tragic loss feelings of dismay and respect intermingled with battle-torn nerves. But by 4.30 pm they had scrambled once again. Leading the seven Spitfires over a destroyer being attacked near Dover, Flt Lt Ellis climbed to intercept a gaggle of Messerschmitts who were escort to JU87 Stukas. A typical free-for-all dog-fight ensued with No 610 squadron fighting with a new-found strength and determination. Quite often the fear of death was overcome by rashness even to the point of foolhardiness. They gave no quarter and within minutes they had brought down five enemy machines, the rest fleeing to the French coast at sea level.

On 27th July, No 501 squadron came down to Hawkinge from Gravesend. Visibility was poor, the sky grey and overcast when Flt Lt Cox unwittingly became the target of Dover guns. His Hurricane was hit with the first salvo of shells. Cox was unable to extricate himself from the blazing cockpit before his aircraft dived into the sea. Our gunners, ever vigilant, often confused by dozens of unidentifiable, twisting blurred shapes at varying heights, speeds and angles of incidence, would put up a formidable barrage of lethal explosives.

Flt Lt Don McKay, however, returned jubilant. He was awarded a 'probable' by the station Intelligence Officer for severely damaging a Stuka. For the third day running No 501 squadron put up their first patrol on 29th at 07.20 hrs. Successfully vectored to intercept over forty Stukas and Bf 109s, McKay, leading 'A' Flight, put a Stuka down almost immediately which brought his total of enemy aircraft destroyed to five.

As the No 501 pilots were climbing out of their cockpits a Hurricane of No 43 squadron, piloted by Plt Off K. C. Campbell tried desperately to make some kind of landing. But because of extensive damage to the vital flaps and ailerons the unwieldy aircraft overshot. The Hurricane crashed at Elham, and when the groundcrew arrived at the scene they found Campbell dead in his cockpit.

CHAPTER EIGHT

'Engage Target ... Engage Target' August 1940 - October 1940

In August Goering decided to smash our front-line aerodromes which brought Hawkinge under attack for the first time in its history. It had received attention many times in the twenties and thirties when biplanes of the Auxiliary squadrons had whirled and dived in a spectacle of peace-time war-gaming. If little had been achieved then at least it drew young men to the recruiting offices. Nevertheless, the airfield, village and surrounding area were now to receive a new and somewhat terrifying experience, when live High Explosive bombs were dropped across the length and breadth of the front-line base. Incendiaries were to splutter a fierce yellow while buildings collapsed with a deafening roar and unfamiliar aero-engines screamed overhead. Windows shattered, doors blew out and roofs caved in. Earth and stone heaved while smoke, black and thick, billowed and spiralled aloft blotting out the sun in a man-made eclipse.

On the Sunday before the first attack, Hitler's Luftwaffe were out in force over the Dover area, shooting down barrage balloons in an attempt to attract our fighters away from other areas. Something like eleven RAF fighter squadrons were engaged throughout the day's proceedings.

It was a little after lunch when a red flare shot into the sky above the Flying Control Room. From low cloud the sound of a Merlin engine crackled and spat as the throttle control was opened. Appearing suddenly through the cloud a Hurricane, with little speed to speak of, approached to land. The pilot saw the bulk of the hangars just in time to pull the nose of his machine up. He managed to remain aloft for his second attempt at landing. This next attempt was in no way better than the first. The Hurricane bucked and veered and the engine was about to falter. Exceptionally low for any drastic change in direction, Plt Off McLintoch put the nose down in sheer desperation. It was a case of now or never. The Hurricane dropped like a brick and caught its tail wheel in the perimeter fence. Airmen who stood watching McLintoch's arrival saw the aircraft turn over in a complete somersault before it buried its engine compartment in soft ground. No 615 squadron had lost another of its aircraft.

Across the English Channel on Monday 12th August, some fifty or so miles inland, the Luftwaffe prepared for the day's events. German ground crews had been up early servicing the Messerschmitt Me 110s and Bf 109s of the 'Experimental Gruppe 210'. This special unit had been operating for about month using fighters both twin- and single-engined, carrying bombs fitted to improvised racks under the wings. It began as an attempt to prove that fighter aircraft could hit targets equal to the normal bomber units with

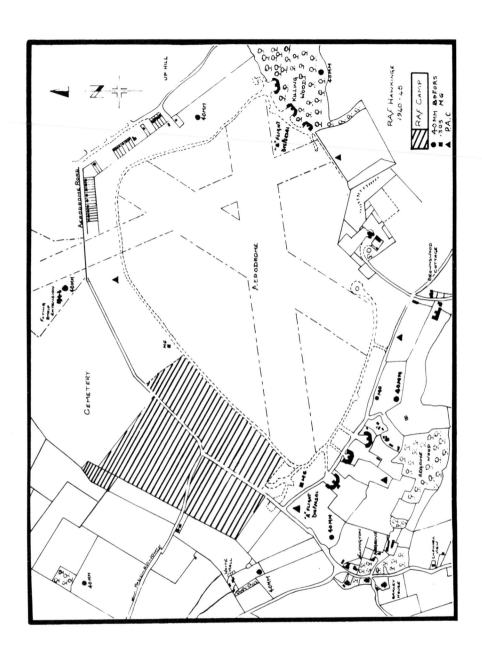

RAF HAWKINGE
1940-45

RAF CAMP

40MM BOFORS
.303 MG
P.A.C

the added advantage of reverting to the fighter role afterwards. Carrying either 500 lb or 1,000 lb bombs they had already been successful in attacking convoys in the Channel and were now to extend their role in attacking radar stations and forward airfields.

Fighter Command was to experience its most intense day since the war began. This was the beginning of Reichmarshal Goering's fierce attacks in the South East, attacks which were aimed at softening up our airfields in preparation for Hitler's 'Adler Tag' offensive due to start on 13th.

By 06.00 hrs the briefing rooms were packed with German bomber and fighter crews listening to their orders. Outside, under trees and around the aerodrome boundary, stood the Zerstorer ME 110s and the Bf 109s, now armed with their respective bomb loads of HE, incendiaries and delayed-action mines. At every airfield from Le Mans to Antwerp, the story was the same. Crews and machines waited for action.

The attacks on 12th were divided into five separate phases which moved from East to West and back again. The first raid of the day began over Dover at 07.30 hrs. By 09.00 hrs five radar stations were under attack. Dunkirk near Faversham received a pounding but the massive pylons remained standing. At Dover the large aerial towers which had goaded the Germans from their high vantage just behind the Castle remained standing after an attack, although wooden huts inside the compound were smashed to pulp.

There was a lapse of one hour before further raids began and this, the second phase, was concentrated in the Southampton and Portsmouth areas. At 13.25 hrs a formation of Do 17Zs came in to attack Manston, the forward airfield near Ramsgate. It was the first of many such raids on that particular airfield which later proved so devastating.

At Hawkinge the station personnel were gloomy. Roused by the Tannoy at the unearthly hour of 05.00 hrs, they had reluctantly crawled from their beds and, as the mists rose slowly from the turf, they began to flit between the buildings. Gradually the station came to life. Breakfast over, the airmen were seen sauntering towards dispersals where the huts were to be cleaned ready for the next squadron's arrival. The starter batteries stood in their sandbagged emplacements. The Buffs manning the machine gun nests blew into their hands as they waited for the tea-urn to arrive. Most of them had only fired a few rounds of ammunition into the butts at Lydden Spout before being split into three groups for airfield defence. The only excitement of their service, so far, was shouting 'Who goes there?' to young airmen returning from clandestine courtships invading the perimeter fences at night. The young Buffs took great delight in marching these captured swains to the guardroom at rifle point.

At 07.40 hrs, the Observer Corps post at Dover Castle reported seeing large formations of enemy aircraft heading in towards them. The sky became filled with aircraft stretching from Deal to Dungeness at about

10,000 feet. Within minutes of the enemy being sighted No 610 squadron scrambled from Biggin Hill. No 23 squadron Hurricanes were left behind on 'stand-by' and, as the pilots sat in their cockpits eager to join the fray, the 610 Spitfires were heavily engaged in individual dog-fights over the whole of the Romney Marsh area with the German fighter-bombers, commanded by Lt Rossigner, attacking the Rye radar station.

At 09.30 hrs, fifteen Do 17Zs of 1/KG2, under the command of Major Outzmann, released over one hundred and forty bombs upon Lympne, ripping the turf to shreds and smashing all the hangars. By 10.00 hrs Bentley Priory, the heart of Fighter Command, was a hive of activity. The plotting tables became covered with coloured discs and markers which mingled in one large kaleidoscope as they were pushed about by the WAAF croupiers. Over the South East the sound of aircraft was everywhere. The drone of high flying bombers became a back-cloth to the high pitched scream of crippled machines as they plummeted to earth out of control. The snarl of fighter engines under full boost turning, diving, climbing — and the incessant chatter of machine guns added to the confusion. Now and again a stricken German bomber, wheels down and trailing smoke, would race at rooftop height towards the Channel harassed by a lone British fighter hellbent on its destruction.

At noon the Hurricanes of No 32 squadron were ordered to Hawkinge. Sqdn Ldr M. Crossley, DFC, who had joined the squadron before the war, was now commanding them. He already had seven confirmed victories. At the airfield the pilots lay on the grass in groups watching the vapour trails strung across the sky. By now five radar stations had been put out of action temporarily, two convoys in the Thames Estuary had been dive-bombed and Portsmouth had been heavily attacked. It was 14.30 hrs before the pilots were galvanised into action. With the jangling bell still ringing in their ears they ran for their aircraft, donning their parachute packs. Starter leads were already plugged into the engines when the green Very-Light spluttered into the air. Starter buttons were pushed almost simultaneously. As the Hurricanes left the grass, No 610 were on the way back to refuel. By keeping at least one squadron in the air on patrol, Air Marshal Keith Park was able to intercept any likely raiders. The Observer Corps were now the only reliable means of reporting enemy formations.

After an uneventful patrol No 32 returned to refuel. The petrol bowsers with their earth pins trailing along behind were trundling back to the fuel dump when the next scramble signal was given. The Hurricane engines, already hot from their previous patrol, burst into life once more and each gradually became absorbed into a vast unsynchronised pulsating noise. They left the grass about half way down the airfield, rocking slightly as the pilots pumped their undercarriages up.

Mike Crossley recalls an incident during one of these rapid take-offs.

"On one occasion one of the pilots, a sergeant called Henson, got so excited rushing to catch up with the others that he pushed off the gun button safety catch, caught his glove in it and loosed off a broadside which smashed a row of windows in a hangar!"

However, one Hurricane remained sitting firmly on the grass near Killing Wood dispersal, looking forlorn and helpless with its engine cover removed. With an arm reaching into the complicated machinery an airman balanced on the wing root while another stood by taking the full measure of wrath from the irate pilot.

Thirty minutes had elapsed. The pilot had long since walked back to the dispersal hut and the two airmen, now engrossed in technicalities, failed to hear the drone of unfamiliar aero engines.

At about 16.45 hrs, fifteen JU88s of II/KG76 were observed forming up over the French coast. No 32 squadron were in the Margate area when the JU88s were hurtling over the Channel towards Dungeness. Three miles from Dymchurch the German formation split into two separate groups both maintaining a height of 5,000 feet. One group continued inland heading for Lympne, while the other turned parallel with the coast until reaching a position opposite Sandgate where it altered course to Hawkinge. At the first snarl of the twin Jumo engines under full boost, the two mechanics ran from the Hurricane to the nearest slit trench. No warning had been given and the airfield personnel were taken by complete surprise.

Signalman Harvey, of 2nd London Infantry Brigade, was sitting in a trench fiddling with his wireless set trying to raise Brigade HQ. His earphones muffled the sound of hostile aero engines and the first he knew of what was happening was when huge clods of earth straddled his trench. Airmen and civilians dived or fell into nearby trenches and dugouts. The station electrician, for most of the time the raid was in progress, was trying to recover from his head-splitting descent to the bottom of a very deep trench. To add to his dilemma he was pinned down by the weight of a burly airman who refused to budge an inch.

The first wave of three machines, in line abreast, released their bombs too early for a mixture of HEs and incendiaries ploughd into the ground from a point in the centre of the field to the tarmac in front of the hangars. As the first wave screamed overhead a solitary Hispano cannon, from somewhere near the fuel dump, opened fire, spraying the sky like a garden hose. The next three were most accurate, their bombs falling among the station buildings. The large workshop disappeared in a huge sheet of flame and smoke. Engine parts, tools and sundry bits of bent and twisted metal hurled through the air with terrible force. No 3 hangar received direct hits through the roof causing two of the massive iron doors to buckle and collapse trapping two civilians and an airman.

The main equipment store also received a direct hit. The building seemed to erupt from the inside showering the air with burning clothing and boxes. Two houses, formerly used by married personnel but now used to billet airmen, were blown to pieces killing and wounding the inhabitants. Ammunition stored in one corner of the bombed hangar began to explode sending bullets, some of them tracers, in all directions. Each bomb explosion produced a sound wave that reverberated against the sides of the hangar. The successive detonations produced a cacophony of blast, echo, blast effect. The ground shook and trembled underfoot, paving slabs cracked and telephone wires snapped as poles were uprooted. Trees shed their leaves. The last of the bombers leaving chaos in its wake disappeared into the haze its engines pouring blue vapour.

The duty section of 'E' Company Buffs had been detailed to sleep in a hastily acquired chicken hut near the Gibraltar Lane area and, although it had been scrubbed out several times, the smell persisted. Then only eighteen years of age, Pte Ron Cook recalls, "I was delivering a message from our Company HQ, to the RAF HQ, when the raid started. Not wanting to be caught out in the open I naturally dived into the nearest shelter. There were already a number of 'bodies' down there but as it was pitch dark I had no idea who they were. I could hear the crump, crump of exploding bombs then someone quite close to me said,'What are you doing here? . . . don't you know this shelter is for officers only!' I could only stammer a reply which explained why I happened to be there. But I was told, in no uncertain terms, 'All right, you can stay now, but don't let it happen again!' "

Marion McNeill, a WAAF wireless operator recalled, "I remember my first sight of the German aircraft, visible from the side windows of the house. Our wireless receivers were on wooden trestle tables quite close to the windows. I saw quite clearly the black crosses on the aircraft and watched the bombs falling. I happened to be on their particular radio frequency at the time and heard 'Sieg Heil! Sieg Heil!' and something else which sounded like 'Bomben!', although I was not quite sure of everything they said as my German was largely academic. I had never been to Germany."

It was all over in minutes. Billowing clouds of smoke and dust hung in the air like a huge black shroud. White-hot metal and stones sizzled on the ground everywhere. There was silence for a time. Even the birds had stopped singing. Then, as if by some prearranged signal, blue-overalled airmen appeared from the trenches. Some stood and stared at the absolute shambles around them, while others, bewildered and stunned by the crash of bombs, shook their heads vigorously.

Cautiously the airmen picked their way through the maze of bomb craters edged with chalk and smouldering miniature volcanoes. The station ambulance, a 30-cwt Bedford, its roof covered with earth, made its way slowly towards the collapsed buildings over roads littered with debris. Close to the Watch Office a small van burned fiercely and a tree lay torn from the ground, its roots staring up at the blackened sky.

Soldiers were alredy helping to free the trapped civilians from the collapsed door section. Through the gaping, twisted opening there could be seen a wing burning. The red, white and blue roundel hung in blistered shreds. Trestles and wooden steps were smashed to matchwood, an anvil torn from its bench had been hurled with sickening force at a starter battery where it had become embedded. The fire truck and crash tender arrived and were soon bereft of their hatchets, hoses and foam cylinders. Water cascaded over the burning scene, foam engulfed the little van, its tyres now a black mass of smouldering rubber, its smashed windscreen littering the ground around it.

Miraculously the Watch Office and Flying Control had remained unscathed and although the telephone system was inoperable, the wireless network was still working. No 32 squadron, now low on fuel and out of ammunition also after their brush with Bf 109s just east of Dover, broke off their combat and made for home. Some of them went inland and were able to land at Biggin Hill, but five came in to land at the airfield. They appeared over the village in line astern and Mike Crossley, knowing his brood were unable to go much further, told the controller it was Hawkinge or bust! He received an apologetic reply with instructions to avoid the many craters which dotted the field. Undercarriages locked down, the Hurricanes prepared to land anxiously watched by those below, for no one at that time knew if unexploded bombs were on the field. Unwilling to tempt fate too much the five pilots seemed to put their aircraft down gently. As the last machine rolled to a stop everyone gave a sigh of relief. Normally the ground crews would be out to their aircraft at once but everyone was otherwise engaged dealing with the chaos.

The Hurricane pilots stepped down from their machines and began to take off their parachutes, when a small formation of twin-engined aircraft appeared from the north east. As the first bullets were being fired from the nose guns of the raiders, ground personnel dived for cover once again. Bombs exploded simultaneously with the sound of the Tannoy blaring out a warning to take cover. No 5 hangar erupted, showering the village with bricks, tiles and timber. This second attack by the same unit was, like the first one, over in a few minutes. The JU88s sped out over Folkestone towards the sea unhindered. It was some considerable time before anyone stirred from their shelters and trenches. When they did eventually emerge they found that although incendiaries were burning and spluttering all over the place, not one of the Hurricanes had been damaged. The greater part of No 5 hangar was, however, a heap of rubble.

Robert Fry, of the Folkestone Auxiliary Fire Service, remembers they were still a comparatively untried force, regarded by many with a degree of tolerance and amusement, especially by members of the regular Fire Brigade. When they answered the call for assistance from the airfield they were greeted with cheers.

"It was a chaotic scene which greeted us," Robert recalls, "there were fires in several places. The water tower supplying the pressure for hydrants had been holed by bomb splinters in many places. Water cascaded from it reducing our mains supply to a mere trickle. We found a sunken static water tank close to a burning hangar. To reach it we were forced to remove sections of iron railings and cut down small ornamental trees. Along the top of the railings ran a number of stout electrical cables. I remember a chap called Rumsey was with me at the time. He shouted, 'What shall I do with these?' 'Cut them!' I replied. He did. Later a weary soldier came by with a Signals flash on his shoulder and found the severed cable ends. His language was to be heard to be believed. 'What . . . fool cut the communications to the guns?!', he roared. George and I looked at each other in silence but thought it was not the time to confess."

The firemen were troubled by a constant series of small explosions and found the cause to be a small arms cache burning. Belts of .303 ammunition were going off in the intense heat.

"We kept the hoses spread throughout the wreckage all night," Robert said. "Amongst the debris were a couple of Hurricane fighters — undamaged too, but no attempt to salvage them could be made until morning. Our priority was to get RAF Hawkinge operational as soon as possible. A mobile canteen performed the impossible supplying endless tea and sandwiches almost non-stop. In the dawn light we left the airfield. Later, when we sat down for a well-earned breakfast, we had that unmistakable feeling that we had at last become firemen."

The task of filling bomb craters began that day. Parties of airmen had been working throughout the night to shift tons of rubble which had blocked the roads. Windows were boarded and walls, scarred and cracked, were shored temporarily. Aerodrome Road was like a canal in parts where the water,used to fight the fires, had run down to find its level. Troops arrived from Shorncliffe Camp to assist with the clearing operation. A young subaltern was in charge. Obtaining a Lewis machine gun from the armoury he vowed, "I'll get a Jerry if he shows himself!" In fact he very nearly succeeded in getting Flg Off Brooker's Hurricane which crashed on the airfield at 4.30 pm.

On the 14th, Plt Offs Smythe and Barton had both brought their damaged aircraft back to Hawkinge and were following the circuit ready to land when the young subaltern raised the heavy Lewis. He would have fired but for the timely shout of 'They're ours!' Both Hurricanes, unable to lower their undercarriages and at near stalling speed dropped on to the grass in a cloud of dust. No 615 squadron were down that day and lost two pilots, Flg Off Collard and Plt Off Montgomery. Flg Off Gayner managed to bring his damaged Hurricane back after shooting it out with an ME 110.

Thursday 15th broke fine and warm with just a slight haze to upset visibility over the Channel. It enabled the Luftwaffe to exert its biggest attack of the Adler Tag offensive, using every fighter, bomber and dive-bomber they could lay their hands on. Manston had received such a terrible

Hurricanes of No 501 squadron taking off from Hawkinge in August 1940. Both these aircraft were later shot down 18th August 1940, by Oberleutnant Schoepfel of JG26. Plt Off K. N. T. Lee baled out wounded from SD–N, and Plt Off J. W. Bland was killed in SD–T.

(Imperial War Museum)

pounding the previous day that four of its hangars were reduced to rubble.

The first attacks of the day were made on Lympne and Hawkinge. It had been a quiet morning with just the usual reconnaissance flights operating and the arrival of army trucks loaded with soldiers who were to put the finishing touches to the battered turf.

No 501 squadron had already arrived and their Hurricanes were standing at dispersal. The pilots were scanning the sky as they lounged in basket-weave chairs. One or two were lying on the grass using their Mae-Wests as a pillow, until they were told to put them on by the Flying Officer Discipline!

On the other side of the English Channel at Bonningues, near Calais, the Luftwaffe chief of staff of the 2nd Flying Corps, Oberst Paul Diechman, prepared to send off his first sorties of over one hundred aircraft. At 11.00 hrs the armada, consisting of sixty JU87s heavily escorted by Bf 109s, left the coast of France to be spotted by our radar. The Stukas of II/ST/G1, under the command of Hauptmann Keil, were to attack Lympne with their 500 and 250 kilo bombs. Over two dozen Stukas of IV/ST/LG1, commanded by Hauptmann von Brauchitsch, headed for Hawkinge similarly loaded. Above them, weaving and wheeling in loose formation, were the Bf 109s of JG26, led by Adolf Galland, already a famous German fighter ace.

The Hurricane pilots were scrambled.

115

Just north of the aerodrome an old horse-drawn binder clattered round a cornfield, its mechanism spewing forth corn stooks. By this time the Stuka Gruppen had come within range of the Dover guns. Keil's Stukas headed for Lympne, while the other group continued inland out of range of the shells. Brauchitsch's formation turned towards Hawkinge. Arthur Edney had stopped to repair his ailing binder. Engrossed in unravelling the tangled twine he failed to hear the approaching dive-bombers until they were over Swingfield. The frightening crash of Bofors guns defending the airfield burst upon him. As Arthur looked up the gull-winged raiders began their descent. The screaming, snarling engines merged with the thunder of exploding bombs, most of which, due to the formidable barrage, were released too soon. Bombs went astray and fell into the Rheindene Wood on the outskirts of the village, others straddled the cemetery and open fields to the North. But vital electric cables were severed in several places which put the Dover radar system out of action for a time.

At the first crash of gunfire, airmen in the village barber shop dived for cover, and were soon piled on top of each other under the stairs. Eric Haddow, in white apron and scissors poised, was bowled over by the rush. Having a bath at the Haddows was considered a luxury. Eric saw one young airman, clad only in a bath towel, rush out of the front door into the main road. The Reverend Thomas had toiled for hours with bucket and spade to construct a shelter near the church. When an accurate stick of bombs blasted No 2 hangar the village streets became alive with hot shrapnel and bullets. The vicar, his Panama hat rammed over his ears, was unceremoniously bundled into his shelter. His steel helmet given to him by the local ARP (he scorned its use) hastily abandoned in the rush, rolled down the centre of the road.

At the time of the second raid Marion McNeill was walking down Aerodrome Road towards the NAAFI when she heard the sound of aircraft. She recalled:

"I looked up and there were the Stukas approaching — I remember that scream they made as they performed a most graceful curve and started their dive — it was really nerve-shattering. I remember grabbing at a poor Army boy who was on sentry duty quite near the cemetery gates and where a road block had been erected. Together we dived to the ground between a tree and a wall. Something exploded quite near us — we were suddenly bombarded with clods of earth and eventually covered with decanted foul-smelling pond water."

Marion and the soldier remained there until the raid subsided. She continued the story.

"We both stood up and brushed ourselves down as best we could. I asked him where the nearest shelter was — he pointed towards the aerodrome and gave me directions. Feeling rather nervous I found it and went inside. At the rear of the shelter were about fifteen or so young boys in uniform. RAF or

Army I cannot quite remember, but I know there was a sergeant in charge. Their faces were, I distinctly remember, literally green!"

'E' Block used by sergeants disappeared in smoke and flames covering the nearby slit trenches with earth and rubble. The Bofors guns failed to find a target but Nos 501 and 54 squadrons had already attacked the fleeing raiders near Lympne, and were now heading towards Hawkinge. They caught the Stukas as they climbed out of their dives. One of them, piloted by Lt von Rosen, was shot down and both he and his gunner perished in the crash. Sgt N. A. Lawrence, of No 54 squadron, got two Stukas and then was himself shot down in the sea off Folkestone. Another Stuka was shot down by Sgt Farnes of No 501 squadron, and the next went down under the guns of Sgt McKay. Flt Lts A. R. Putt and J. A. A. Gibson, both of the same squadron, lost their Hurricanes to the Messerschmitt escort, baling out over Folkestone. One other Stuka, destroyed by the fire of many guns flew into electric cables near Cheriton and partly demolished a house.

The airfield at Lympne had received an even worse battering. Water and power supplies had been cut and not one solitary building stood unscathed. Used mainly for emergency landings and the less important of the two airfields it was reduced to rubble. Hawkinge, on the other hand, survived once again, although Luftwaffe sources claimed to have completely destroyed both airfields. This tendency to attack less important airfields not in Fighter Command resulted in such places as Eastchurch, Ford and Detling receiving devastating raids.

That afternoon the radar plots were so numerous that the whole picture of operations became confused. Eleven of our fighter squadrons, something like 130 Hurricanes and Spitfires, were scrambled to intercept the enemy. No 32 squadron had been despatched to Hawkinge immediately after the morning raid and, by 14.30 hrs the pilots were sitting in their cockpits on 'stand by', apprehensively considering the possibility of being attacked on the ground. Within twenty minutes they were flying over the village towards Harwich. Once again the airfield was without a fighter squadron for protection. As the scattered trolley batteries were being gathered from the field the Tannoy speakers gave a loud clicking sound which was followed by someone shouting into the microphone, 'Take shelter! Take shelter!' The Tannoy switched off with a metallic clunking sound. Then the now familiar droning sound of enemy aircraft could be heard. Above the airfield at about 10,000 feet were about twenty HE 111s and DO 17s, slowly moving towards the Channel coast. The guns opened fire. Black puffs began to dot the sky as the shells exploded, the green nose-cones of the shells fell to bounce from village roof tiles as the bombs began to rain down upon the already crater-scarred airfield. Crump! Crump! The bombs fell in straight lines across the airfield and up onto the North Downs, over the other side and across fields towards Cheriton. Airmen were huddled together in trenches like rabbits in a burrow. The language was foul as they shouted abuse to the heavens.

This massive full-scale air offensive on the RAF continued until 20.00 hrs in the evening with over 2,000 German aircraft involved. It was an all out effort to smash Fighter Command. It failed.

On 16th, the Luftwaffe were up again in the South East but they avoided Hawkinge. This short gap in enemy activity allowed work filling in bomb craters which had sunk overnight. The turf looked more like a vast patchwork of brown and white mounds as if they had been made by giant moles. Local Defence Volunteers and civilians of every description set to with picks and shovels. A steam roller, complete with Lewis machine gun mounted on the roof, ventured out to flatten the mounds while visiting pilots snatched a meal and took a cat-nap. Food and sleep were becoming luxuries.

Sqdn Ldr Arnold, who had arrived early that morning to take over as Station C.O., watched the arrival of No 111 squadron Hurricanes. They were to lose two of them before lunch. Flt Lt Ferris was killed when he collided with a Dornier over Marden. Five minutes later Sgt Carnell was forced to bale out over Dungeness severely wounded. No 610 squadron came down to relieve them and by 17.00 hrs had lost Flt Lt Warner.

Three days later No 615 squadron Hurricanes came to the airfield to operate Channel interceptions and by 12.40, on this beautiful Sunday, they were scrambled towards Dover. Even before Dover was reached they received a course correction towards the Thames Estuary. Hawkinge lay far to the South West when, at slightly less than 20,000 feet, they were attacked by Bf 109s. The first of the twelve Hurricanes to be hit was a reserve machine which had the distinction of being built in the very first batch of fifty. Pilot Officer Looker, overcoming a constant stream of difficulties, eventually landed at Croydon. His action contributed to the preservation of that particular Hurricane which is now on display in the London Science Museum.

While Looker was battling with his damaged machine the airfield received another attack. This was also the day when No 501 squadron were to lose six of their Hurricanes in the space of five hours.

The first Hurricane of the squadron lost on that day was flown by Flg Off R. L. Dafforn who baled out near Biggin Hill at about 12.00 hrs.

The dew-soaked grass at the airfield covered by ground mist played havoc with the guns. The crews constantly wiped dry the sights and breech mechanism. By midday the sun had disappeared behind cloud and although the red alert had been in operation since early morning the Tannoy suddenly blared out its warning. At 13.15 hrs the telephone rang in the control office. The Observer Corps at Dover had seen a small formation of enemy aircraft heading in towards Folkestone. Whistles blew from the furthermost corners of the airfield. Airmen took shelter quickly. It was becoming second nature to them now. White-aproned cooks ran into their dugout carrying the inevitable tea canister. The post corporal dived from his bicycle into a convenient hedge. But strange as it may seem the petrol bowser crew stood their ground.

118

The sector controller at Biggin Hill sent No 615 squadron towards Hawkinge to intercept the intruders. Nos 32 and 610 squadrons were at 'stand-by' on the ground at Biggin, while No 501 were patrolling the coast near Margate. Within five minutes of the telephone call, six DO 17Zs came over the village roofs at no more than 200 feet. They were escorted by Bf 109s. Bullets and cannon shells ripped into the sodden turf from the village to Elvington Lane. The bowser crew threw themselves to the ground, half expecting to be engulfed in flames at any minute. The Dorniers roared over the airfield. The fighter escort shot up the gun emplacements. Because of the speed and low-flying the anti-aircraft fire was not effective.

Meanwhile, No 501 squadron Hurricanes had met some Messerschmitts near Canterbury. The first to succumb to the accurate attentions of a Bf 109 flown by Oblt G. Schoepfel, was Sgt Don McKay, who had no alternative but to bale out from his burning aircraft. Plt Off K. N. T. Lee, followed suit when he also came up against the same German pilot. Lee had leg wounds when found and was admitted to hospital. Plt Off F. Kozlowski's Hurricane came in for the same treatment and practically blew up beneath him. Seriously injured Kozlowski was also taken to hospital. Schoepfel brought his guns to bear on another Hurricane flown by Plt Off J. W. Bland. It blew up killing Bland instantly. The sixth victim of the squadron was Flt Lt G. E. B. Stoney who, about four hours later flying over the Thames, was shot down before he knew what had happened. Although he baled out he later died of his injuries.

In just ten days Fighter Command had lost over one hundred fighters in the air and about thirty on the ground. The Luftwaffe were no better off. Aircraft loss was not the biggest danger for the RAF, they were now more concerned with pilot deficiency for we were fast reaching a critical point. We had lost about 154 pilots in those ten days either killed or wounded and, in the same period, replacements were a mere 63 who in the main were only partly trained.

The frightening toll of pilots brought down in the sea subsequently lost through drowning was now very serious. Air Vice-Marshal Arthur Harris was given the task of organising the long neglected Air Sea Rescue service, the need for which had not been foreseen in such dramatic light during our pre-war air exercises. Rescue craft of Coastal Command, boats of the Naval Auxiliary Patrol and RAF launches came under the direct control of the local naval authority. The RAF, however, continued to be responsible for air search techniques and twelve Lysanders, formerly of Army Co-operation squadrons, were sent to various coastal fighter stations. Hawkinge was to share with Manston towards the end of 1940, Lysanders previously serving with No 4 (AC) squadron. It was not until mid-1941 that a permanent flight was to take over rescue duties in a professional sense at Hawkinge.

In the period immediately following the last airfield attack repair crews were busy replacing temporary sheeting to the roof of No 2 hangar. One airman whose concentration was impaired by the arrival of Sgt Corfe's Spitfire very nearly ended up in hospital when he lost his footing. Corfe's aircraft had been badly shot up whilst No 610 squadron were engaging the fighter escort to ME 110s bombing a convoy called 'Totem' in the Dover Straits. Corfe hastily vacated the burning cockpit before the whole aircraft became an inferno. There were now two wreckages to move from the grass field. In the morning a Hurricane of No 32 squadron, piloted by Plt Off Pfeiffer, had attempted to land on one wheel. The one remaining oleo leg collapsed and the aircraft did a neat pirouette. Pfeiffer walked away unhurt but visibly shaken.

It was lucky Hawkinge again on 24th when Manston was attacked twice and so severely that all personnel were immediately evacuated to safer quarters. No 32 squadron received a jolt during these particular raids for they were to lose five fighters that day. Scrambled from the airfield at 10.00 hrs to intercept a heavy raid taking place over Dover, the squadron found themselves ranging over a very wide area of the county at heights of between 2,000 feet and 20,000 feet. Plt Off Pniak was shot up by a Bf 109 and was forced to abandon his Hurricane over the town. His aircraft dived into the sea just outside the breakwater. He floated down to splash into the harbour, where he was found by the crew of a naval launch, calmly sitting astride a buoy. An extremely confident and determined young man, Pniak, a Polish pilot who had joined the squadron only sixteen days before, was back at Hawkinge within the hour and was flying that afternoon when the squadron scrambled. By 16.20 hrs he had been shot up again over Lyminge and fell out of his inverted Hurricane before it crashed on the outskirts of the village. But this time he was wounded and spent the remainder of the month in hospital. Plt Offs R. F. Smythe and E. G. A. Seghers both left their cockpits in a hurry before their Hurricanes crashed in the same area. The last to leave his spinning fighter was the C.O., Sqdn Ldr Mike Crossley.

This top scoring fighter squadron was rested the following day. So far they had earned one DSO and five DFCs, losing five pilots killed and one a prisoner-of-war. Even on their last day in the area they lost two pilots and aircraft. Plt Off J. Rose managed to bale out but Plt Off K. Gillman, unable to extricate himself from the whirling cockpit, perished when it dived into the sea.

Both No 79 and 610 squadrons shared facilities on the 26th. They were sipping mugs of tea from Annie's tea-van when both units were scrambled. Sqdn Ldr Heyworth led his Spitfires of No 79 towards Deal and lost no time in shooting down an HE 59 Seaplane. But at midday over Folkestone it was a different story for the pilots of No 610 who were to lose three of their Spitfires.

Plt Off K. Webster brought his damaged Spitfire over the eastern airfield boundary. Airmen, who had been watching the dog-fight, turned to watch Webster's approach. The undercarriages were down but appeared not to be locked in that position, probably due to loss of hydraulics. As soon as the wheels touched the grass both oleo legs collapsed. The Spitfire somersaulted and burst into flames killing the pilot outright. In the direction of Paddlesworth, to the north west of the airfield, a plume of black smoke spiralled aloft over the crash of another Spitfire which had failed to make the airfield. The group of airmen heard the spluttering of another Merlin engine behind them and swung round just in time to see Sgt P. Else bale out of his damaged Spitfire before it crashed into the side of Castle Hill.

For the past three months Arthur Edney had watched the dog-fights increase in intensity and, outside the comparative safety of his cottage, dodged falling ammunition cases and other debris. He was to remember one incident especially. It happened on the morning of August 28th. Rodney the shire horse stood between the shafts looking slightly contemptuous of the Edney family who, despite rumours of an invasion by Hitler, were making determined efforts to finish haymaking.

The drone of high-flying aircraft and the chatter of machine guns did nothing to disturb the colourful cock pheasants strutting about the hedgerows. They somehow seemed immune from man's hysterical desire to kill one another. Arthur and his two sisters stopped toiling, not because the haycart had reached its capacity but because they heard from above a sound so harsh and unnatural. Suddenly, gyrating windmill fashion, a metallic blur fell from the sky and dived into a crater of its own making. Arthur ran to the crater's edge where a blue vapour hovered like incense. He looked down at the remains of one of Hitler's Messerschmitts which had bored down through fifteen feet of flint stone and clay. A strange smell, a mixture of petrol, engine coolant, burnt harness and cordite invaded his nostrils. He stood back and with indescribable feelings saw the pilot, Oberlt Erich Kircheis, descend towards the village of Denton beneath his silk canopy.

On the following day the airfield gunners were, just after half past six in the evening, scrambling to take up their positions on the Bofors when the warning of a possible attack had been shouted from the Tannoy. Barrels traversed this way and that in the hope of catching a German fighter. But our Hurricanes were everywhere. Sgt Lacey of No 501 squadron, one of the top scoring pilots in Fighter Command, positioned his Hurricane behind an unsuspecting Bf 109 of Stab JG3, almost over the airfield. The gunners were spellbound by the dog-fight. Someone shouted, 'He's got 'im!' They watched, jubilant as Oberlt Floorke baled out but, while the German pilot floated groundwards, Flt Lt Gibson and Sgt Green had to abandon their Hurricanes near the airfield.

Despite heavy losses inflicted on our fighter squadrons we were still able to intercept the Luftwaffe bomber formations. However, Dowding's dilemma of finding enough pilots to fly Fighter Command's fighter reserves was still a critical problem. Most of the replacements had acquired little or no proficiency in combat flying during their abbreviated training and few were to survive any sort of tuition at squadron level. Dowding at the beginning of September, after two months of hard fighting had lost nearly half of his squadron leadership. Those experienced pilots left, upon whom lay the burden of responsibility to survive, suffered physical and mental strains which lessened their efficiency.

On Sunday 1st September the Dover radar stations, after reporting the first signs of enemy raiders, was itself put out of action after one of several heavy raids made on airfields and towns. Enemy formations covered blue sky from Deal to Folkestone. The third and fourth attacks were carried out on Lympne and Hawkinge simultaneously in the late afternoon. It had been a glorious day of sunshine and blue skies but now, as the sun was beginning to change from bright yellow to orange, Messerschmitts screamed over the airfield to shouts of 'Engage Target! Engage Target!' The raiders flew through the polka-dot pattern of Bofors shells unharmed. Reaching Elham they turned back. Now, with the sun's rays in bright shafts of light behind them, they made small obscure targets from which eight bombs fell to smash into buildings. The gunners traversed with the raiders until one of them was hit which blew a sizeable piece from its port wing-tip. When the sound of explosions had died away and while the dust and smoke was settling the German raiders were half way across the Channel towards France.

The Spitfires of no 72 squadron, commanded by Sqdn Ldr Collins, were moved down for the day. They were joined by Wg Cdr Lees, their former C.O., who was taking a day's leave and who thought a day with his old squadron was the best possible way to enjoy it. Before long they were scrambled, and Collins led his unit into a formation of DO 17s who were returning from bombing Eastchurch. In the battle four Spitfires were shot down over Herne Bay, and although the enemy bombers continued on their course, it is known that three crashed in France on landing. Their losses were appalling for only the previous day they had lost Fg Off O. St J. Pigg, and three Spitfires were written off strength. Wg Cdr Lees had joined the melee over Herne Bay and just managed to reach Hawkinge. He crash-landed in a cloud of dust. The crash-tender bumped over the grass to find the pilot trapped in the mangled wreckage. Sgt N. R. Norfolk put his burning Spitfire down at the emergency landing ground at Bekesbourne. The events were nerve-wracking in the extreme. Wg Cdr Lees made sure he would not be left behind when the remnants of 72 were scrambled again in the late afternoon. Eight Spitfires got into the air with the Wg Cdr closely following them in a borrowed and largely patched up aircraft of doubtful efficiency. Flt Lt E. Graham was shot down over Lympne and the Wg Cdr's machine was severely damaged over Dungeness and crashed a second time on the airfield. Sqdn Ldr Collins chased his quarry inland sustaining heavy damage which wrote his aircraft off squadron strength.

It seems inconceivable that the squadron was able to muster aircraft for their tour at Hawkinge on 4th — but they did. Tired and in need of a rest the pilots were continuously engaged in running battles. They lost another three aircraft that day. It was the same story in nearly every fighter squadron. We were down to our last few. The situation was desperate and Air Vice-Marshal Keith Park said so in his written report to Dowding.

On Friday 6th September, Kesselring had sent off an enormous formation of Heinkels, Dorniers and Junkers bombers escorted by Bf 109s.

Feldwebel Werner Gottschalk, with others of II/LG2, took off at 17.30 hrs and set course for the Thames Estuary in his Messerschmitt Bf 109 fighter. Somewhere above Chatham, where the London gun belt began, his aircraft suddenly spun over onto its back. His machine gradually began to lose height so he turned back towards the coast, until near Canterbury, he was attacked by roaming British fighters. He managed to survive by diving into cloud but within sight of the coast his Daimler-Benz engine stopped. Realising his height was insufficient to enable a glide safely across the English Channel, he turned along the ridge of the North Downs looking for a likely place to land. Meanwhile the Flying Control personnel at Hawkinge noticed an unfamiliar aircraft heading towards them with flaps and wheels locked down for a landing.

The light AA Regiment manning the 40 mm Bofors had, like the Buffs manning the machine gun nests, been on RED Alert for most of the past week, half expecting an invasion to occur. Gottschalk, avoiding at all costs the indignity of bailing out over the sea, brought his fighter in to make a perfect landing with a dead engine; something very few German pilots were successful at. The Bf 109 fighter was most difficult to control at low speeds and virtually impossible with a dead engine. The aircraft landed smoothly and trundled along the grass towards the station buildings as if it had every right to be there. But then someone, somewhere, saw and recognised the black Luftwaffe markings on the fuselage and wings. Gottschalk was just leaving the cockpit, carrying his leather flying helmet, when just about every machine gun on the airfield opened fire. He ran towards No 1 hangar where he was met by a soldier who, quite unceremoniously, bundled him inside out of harms way.

Saturday 7th was the Luftwaffe's blitz on London. It was another fine, warm sunny day with just a trace of haze over the Channel. At 11.15 hrs the Luftwaffe had assembled a large force of fighters and behind these ranged at different heights were the bombers. At the cliffs' edge near Cap Griz Nez, stood Reichmarshal Goering with his entourage of generals and colonels to watch his air armada set out on its mission of death and destruction.

At 11.20 hrs an Observer Corps post at Folkestone had spotted a small formation of enemy aircraft clipping the waves to be under the radar screen. They were unable to state the target but warned the airfield nonetheless. From the direction of Sandgate a dozen special fighter bombers, a mixture of Me 110s and Bf 109s, arrived at the airfield at the precise moment the telephone message got through. The first wave of three Bf 109s opened fire on the gun emplacements near Gibraltar Lane. The second wave, this time the twin engined Me 110s, followed in a shallow dive from about 1,000 feet and released their bombs. The HQ building disappeared in a cloud of smoke and debris while trees and a wall collapsed nearby. The next wave straffed the gunsites at Argrove and Terlingham. As they cleared the airfield boundary the final three fighter-bombers made their dive. The first machine made a direct hit on the hostel building which collapsed in a heap of rubble. The second aircraft, upset by the terrific barrage from the now very excited guns, appeared to slide into the attack sideways. It righted itself when over the cemetary gates and, fast running out of target, the pilot released his bombs in the direction of the village. The machine practically stood on its tail as the bombs exploded against two houses at the end of Aerodrome Road. The third machine veered off releasing its bombs in a field at Mill Lane. In the corner of this field was a dugout, built in the First World War. Well preserved over the years, the large oak beams in the roof were stoutly supported by pine logs. Neither had moved or rotted and the whole structure would have withstood considerable battering. But one bomb found its mark and a direct hit on that shelter took six lives.

By now the grass airfield was looking a sorry state due to the combination of recently filled bomb craters, a hot dry summer and crashing fighters. In some areas it was like a dust bowl where large patches of brown dirt mixed with chalk made life difficult. Whirling propellers threw up great clouds of the stuff which covered everything and everybody. Dirt mingled with sweat. It clung to the skin giving a clownish appearance to the hardworking ground crews, who sweated, swore and worked long hours to maintain serviceable aircraft.

September 15th was a day to compare with the 7th. Station personnel waited apprehensively as they watched the hundreds of tell-tale vapour trails increase minute by minute. The softening-up attacks did not materialise. Hitler's invasion plan, operation Sealion, was put back yet again. Had our air force proved invincible? Those watching airmen were not aware that Goering's bomber force had been reduced to twenty machines per squadron instead of thirty. But in any event, large formations of German aircraft still crossed our coast line both by day and night.

It was about this time that Air Vice Marshall Park spoke of certain defects in our defence system. The radar stations, even when operating at their optimum, were usually unable to pinpoint with complete accuracy the height and formation strength. More often than not this information was left to the imagination of the operators. It was because of this lack of precise information that spotter techniques were introduced.

A Spitfire borrowed from No 92 squadron then at Manston, arrived at Hawkinge on 15th September, piloted by Flt Lt A. R. Wright, and flew two sorties on that day. The spotter pilots' job was to climb above enemy formations and collate information about them, such as type of aircraft, how

One of the many Hispano 20mm cannons used round the Hawkinge perimeter to combat enemy attacks. This one covered the south west approaches to the airfield.

(Imperial War Museum)

many, direction and if they split into seperate groups. On Wright's second sortie over Dungeness, he was found by a pair of Bf 109s. Told not to engage the enemy in combat he dived away out of trouble.

In October just three months from the beginning of the Battle of Britain, Goering decided his bomber losses were preventing the air superiority he had hoped for. He decided to introduce the fighter-bomber techniques after the success of the Experimental Gruppe 210 operations. He further ordered that all Jagdgeschwadern were to provide one Staffel each for the new fighter-bomber operations. Subsequently a large number of Bf 109 fighters were fitted with a bomb carrier under the fuselage.

Considering the limited efficiency of our radar units these high flying raiders presented a difficult target to counter. Flying in excess of 25,000 feet the Messerschmitts, using a two-stage supercharger, were far superior in

125

performance to our Spitfire Mk IIas. The RAF's solution was to organise high flying patrols. The lone Spitfires used at Hawkinge in September was the first, but a completely new flight, No 421, formed at Gravesend from No 66 squadron, was to perform these special spotter patrols in pairs.

Four days after Flt Lt Januszewics of No 303 squadron had been killed on the airfield, the station was attacked yet again by the Bf 109E–4Bs who each carried a 500 pound bomb. Six of them raced across the Channel in a headlong rush to avoid detection by radar. It was raining. The gunners had donned their groundsheets and had covered the shell racks. Field cannisters rattled and shook in the three ton lorry which contained the midday meal. The Folkestone siren began to wail. Their meal forgotten the crews raced for their guns as their orders were being shouted. In seconds as shouts of 'Ready' echoed around the airfield, the barrels were traversing in the seaward direction. Even so, they were taken by surprise when the six fighter-bombers, their nose cannons blazing, flew in over the airfield boundary at near nought feet.

The many-coloured unit insignia and yellow tail-fins and engine cowlings, stood out against the grey blotch camouflage and even greyer backcloth of rain sodden clouds. With the familiar shouts of "ON! . . . ON! . . . ON!", the Bofors at the Terlingham emplacements, their barrels at near zero elevation, opened fire. Shells burst through the trees as huge clods of earth were flung into the air from exploding bombs. Four exploded harmlessly within fifty yards of the hangars. The fifth demolished the wooden tower used by No 2 squadron in the thirties. The sixth bomb buried the gun simulator building in a pile of rubble.

The fleeing raiders were intercepted by Spitfires of No 222 squadron. For some unknown reason the raiders had split up, each making his own way back to France. Flg Off E. H. Thomas shot one down near Postling and watched the German pilot set alight to his belly-landed fighter.

The early October frosts edging the leaves along the hedgerows brought a hint of winter. But nature was reluctant to give way to this change so early. Rain gave way to cold winds and fog and overcast skies later folded back to reveal a blue azure canopy reminiscent of the summer.

Plt Off H. R. Allen of No 66 squadron had to be taken from his Spitfire cockpit when it crashed on Friday 11th. His aircraft had sustained a terrific pounding from the cannons of Major Moelders of JG51 and practically broke up on landing.

Throughout October, numerous low-level raids were made on Hawkinge. At lunchtime on the 14th, for example, a Me 110 twin engined fighter-bomber dropped two 500 pounders smack in the centre of the squash court. Half an hour later a single Bf 109 streaked in to plant a 250 pounder among the station buildings. It produced a spectacular fountain from a fractured water main, cut telephone wires and killed one soldier.

The siren at Folkestone gave its customary warning on the bright Sunday

A fine photo of a Spitfire MK XII of No 41 squadron who relieved the resident squadron at Hawkinge who were to reequip with 'Twelves' in 1943. (Imperial War Museum)

morning of October 27th. Gunners were, as ever, vigilant. Binoculars scanned the horizon to identify the many fighters approaching the airfield from all directions. Some had lost contact with their units during dog-fights and were low on fuel and without ammunition. A number of them had wireless troubles. Dampness always seemed to effect the sensitive electrical apparatus when the aircraft were flying in excess of 20,000 feet.

By 11.00 hrs a fairly large formation of light bombers and fighter-bombers crossed the coast near Deal, heading for Margate and Ramsgate. At Hawkinge, the Watch Office personnel were apprehensive as reports came in from those two blitzed towns. Taking advantage of the mass of cumulous cloud which had now materialised, eight Bf 109 fighter-bombers headed towards the airfield. The first to spot them was the Royal Marine 3.7 mm gun battery at Swingfield. The raiders changed course as soon as shells burst near them.

Beneath the black explosive smudges dotting the clouds the gunners waited. The only sound echoing from hillock to hillock was the sound of the brass shell cases which banged against each other as they were thrown into a pile.

But before the gunners knew what was happening the raiders were over the airfield and dropping their bombs. They watched the Camp Post Office erupt, the old officers' mess building take a direct hit and Welsh coal flying into the cemetary. No sooner had the first wave gone with Bofors shells curving behind them than the second wave came in. Bullets and cannon shells ripped into trees and buildings. Through billowing smoke they appeared even lower than the previous wave. In seconds they too were gone. Flames licked lazily around the twisted rafters which protruded from the piles of rubble. Dust settled over everything. Water gushed unchecked from fractured pipes while sparks flew from severed wire which hung from blackened walls.

CHAPTER NINE

The Storm Abated, October 1940–July 1941

The summer storm of fierce aerial battles had, by and large, subsided by the end of October 1940, during which the drama of victory against formidable odds had been an element in national survival. As far as the British were concerned it was a turning point for it was on August 16th 1940 that Goering remarked that no more effort should be wasted on such targets as radar stations. He gave his bomber units the task of attacking RAF airfields. But in stark contradiction Hitler, on September 4th, switched the bombing offensive to London thus enabling Dowding's forward fighter stations to survive. It is all very well in hindsight to say the German air force, despite its lack of radar, should have driven home their superiority over the British. We know they should have firstly destroyed our 'Chain Home' radar towers which would have reduced the RAF fighter squadrons to blindness. Then the forward fighter stations such as Hawkinge could have been overwhelmed with bombs to saturation point. Fortunately the Germans only made tentative attacks and in no real logical order. I think it was a General Lee, an American military attache in London who, on September 15th wrote, " I can't for the life of me puzzle out what the Germans are up to. They have great air power and yet are dissipating it in fruitless and aimless attacks all over England".

The German view of what the British call the 'Battle of Britain' seems never to have existed, for they insist the battles for air superiority went on unabated until about May 1941. Although Hitler prophesied that he would eradicate our cities his own day-bombing methods exposed Goering's bomber formations to quite unbearable losses. This inevitably led to the abandonment of 'Operation Sealion'.

Whichever view is accepted, it is an undisputed fact that RAF Hawkinge, with the Spitfires of the newly formed No 421 Flight, was now able to wage its own retaliatory action. Especially brought into existence in October 1940 on the direct orders of Dowding, from the parent No 66 squadron at Gravesend, its job was to operate high-flying reconnaisance sorties to observe enemy formations. The pilots selected were necessarily experienced and individualistic in their temperament and it was, perhaps, their own brand of individualism that was especially sought after which differed from the team disciplines experienced in the usual fighter squadrons.

Previously flying an assortment of Hurricanes and Spitfires they were delighted when their C.O., Sqdn Ldr C. P. Green, managed to convince higher authority that only the Spitfire was capable of securing success. Nine were initially allocated and on the morning of November 15th they flew

One of the few photographs of a 421 Flight Spitfire, taken at Hawkinge in November 1940. This particular machine coded L–Z–I, was flown by Sqdn Ldr C. P. Green, the C.O.

(Elliott collection)

down to their new base at Hawkinge. This short trip was not without incident when Sgt McKay spotted a lone Do 17z near Folkestone and promptly disposed of it with a five second burst.

During December No 421 Flight was involved in shipping spotter sorties and, although pilots were requested not to engage the enemy, combat reports soon became a feature of their reconnaissance duties bringing to the aerodrome a sense of pride of purpose totally divorced from any previous role. One of the earliest examples involved Plt Off Lawrence who scrambled to intercept a German aircraft off Dover directing the German long range guns at Cap Gris Nez who were hurling shells at the seaside towns. The crew of the German Me 110 were unaware of Lawrence's Spitfire on their tail and perished when their aircraft dived into the Channel.

Although Heinkel 60 seaplanes were normally used by the Luftwaffe for their sea rescue operations they were also being used for reconnaissance purposes. Flt Lt O'Meara recalled the occasion he shot one of these down.

"The presence of an HE60 and its fighter escort approaching Dungeness was given to us by the 'Y' Service unit at Capel Le Ferne direct by telephone link instead of going through the usual route via the sector control at Biggin Hill. I remember being in an awful hurry and took off in the nearest aircraft available. It was a blue-painted Spitfire originally used for the early high-flying patrols and had specially fitted bulges in the cockpit canopy to give better pilot visibility. However, I arrived in the area plotted by 'Y' and found the Heinkel without much difficulty. I never really thought about the possibility of a fighter escort and went in from the beam. I watched it fall into the sea then raced back. I seem to recollect I had been in the air for only fourteen minutes. When I stepped out of the aircraft a rigger told me that sector had just sent through a message to intercept!"

Towards the end of December the reconnaissance patrols, always in pairs, were being intercepted more frequently. Both Lawrence and McKay were bounced by Bf 109s one morning near Deal whilst still climbing. While Lawrence was baling out of his burning Spitfire McKay managed to send one of the Messerschmitts into the sea off Sandgate. Lawrence broke a leg

130

leaving the cockpit and was eventually picked up by the Ramsgate lifeboat.

A recently serviced Spitfire stood at 'A' Flight dispersal one morning when a young eighteen-year-old rigger, nicknamed 'Texas', climbed into the cockpit. It was a usual routine for riggers to move aircraft from one position to another which saved bothering pilots on such menial tasks. Texas fired the cartridge starter. The Merlin engine spluttered into life. After the engine had warmed up sufficiently the Spitfire began to move quite leisurely although haphazardly, down a gentle slope onto the airfield. With a roar the aircraft suddenly gathered speed as the throttle control was opened.

The gunners, ever watchful, paid little heed. To them it was just another Spitfire being moved. The Watch Office and Flying Control personnel however, were baffled and asked each other for confirmation. Unauthorised movements fouled-up airfield discipline.

"Who's scrambling?" someone asked.

Texas had one ambition, that of becoming a fighter pilot, but his frequent requests were always turned down by the C.O., with a firm NO!

A further burst of power shot the aircraft bouncing across the grass. Then the inevitable happened. Not trimmed for take off and the propeller in fine pitch, the Spitfire, in an agonising screech of tortured metal, up ended, tearing the starboard wing off. When the dust had settled and with only a cut hand to show for his misdeed, Texas climbed down from the cockpit. He stood back inconspicuously with the gathering crowd of airmen, regaining what composure he could under the circumstances. Amidst babbling voices all asking for the pilot he turned to slink away into obscurity. But this was not to be. He wished the ground would open up and swallow his six-foot frame when a Flt Lt, red-faced and near to apoplexy, screamed at the disillusioned rigger.

"What the hell do you think you were doing?!"

Under escort Texas was marched to the guardroom. It was here he received the biggest dressing down of his life when the C.O. entered into a fearful tirade. At his subsequent and inevitable Court Martial, Texas received a six months' sentence. But, if his escapade had not been enough he was further to astound everybody by escaping from the guardroom the day prior to his removal to the dreaded 'glasshouse'. The only people to make light of the whole affair were the national press who referred to the popular song of the time — If I Only Had Wings'.

The remarkable proficiency in aircraft identification attained by the gunners defending the airfield suddenly took a turn for the worse when, at about 11.00 am, on a dull November morning, they blotted their copybook. A thin, twin-tailed, twin-engined aircraft arrived unannounced over the aerodrome at about 200 feet and proceeded to make the usual left-hand circuit approach to land. The gunners, however, were rather quick off the mark and, although the red alert had not been given, they opened up with well-placed salvos. The twin-tailed visitor veered away, dived to hedgetop height with its undercarriage retracting furiously and flew further inland. Of course, at the first crash of gunfire airmen ran for shelter diving headlong into slit trenches and under hedges. A civilian electrician engaged in repairing power lines stood clasping a mug of hot tea. Amidst the confusion he found himself at the bottom of a nearby trench minus his tea.

Several hits had been observed on the aircraft before it veered away. As a green Very Light shot into the air the gunners were busy congratulating themselves. But their back-slapping was shortlived. Hurried telephone calls were made to the gun emplacements where an embarrassed Lieutenant tried to explain the striking similarity between a Hampden and a Dornier 17Z.

Flt Lt R. A. B. Learoyd had taken part in a raid on the night of 12th/13th August 1940, along with four other Hampdens of No 49 and No 83 squadrons who were to attack an aqueduct forming part of the Dortmund-Emms canal. The first two aircraft were shot down before they were able to release their bomb load. The second two were badly shot up by the murderously accurate flak defences and veered away from the target crippled. The fifth aircraft, piloted by Learoyd, flew to within 150 feet of the target in the face of intense flak and blinding searchlights to release his bombs at the base of the aqueduct. His Hampden, struck many times, climbed into the clouds and made good its escape. Avoiding pursuing nightfighters, Learoyd brought the aircraft and its crew back thus earning himself the highest award for gallantry — the Victoria Cross.

Learoyd was enjoying a few days' holiday with fellow officers in Blackpool. It had been arranged that, on the day in question, a pilot would 'ferry' a Hampden to Blackpool where his friends were due to spend a few more days. Learoyd would then fly the aircraft to Hawkinge en route to the presentation of the Honorary Freedom of his then home town of New Romney. He flew over new Romney where the usual procedure on these occasions was to fly around his mother's house a couple of times to signal his arrival. The flight had been cleared, or so he thought, and he handled the controls with the original pilot sitting on the mainspar behind the pilot's seat with the regular crew in their correct positions.

Passing over Ashford he lost height and arrived over the house at no more than about one hundred feet, did three circuits and flew straight to Hawkinge. He recalled, some thirty or so years later:

"It was a damned silly thing to do. But being stationed in Lincolnshire I had not realised how understandably trigger-happy they were in the south."

During the whole time he was flying round the house and all the way to Hawkinge, he had been subjected to smallarms fire but knew nothing of it at the time. Apparently, the Colonel in charge of the local anti-aircraft units was in the house and was the recipient of some rather heartfelt and urgent pleas from Learoyd's mother to do something about it.

However, reaching Hawkinge airfield he lowered the wheels and prepared to land. Then, whilst in circuit he happened to look out to see a number of small black puffs. By the time he realised what they signified the gunners had found their range and the Hampden was hit a few times. The pilot sitting behind Learoyd received a lump of metal in a leg when the instrument panel more or less disintegrated. Retracting the wheels quickly, Learoyd dived to hedge height and opened the throttles. He eventually landed at West Malling and scrounging a car, sped to New Romney for the presentation ceremony where, somewhat impressed by the accuracy of the defences, he recounted his experiences.

The sequel to the whole day's events was that although the Hampden had been hit no less than 32 times, mostly by machine gun fire, an inquiry later held at Dover Castle, tried to ascertain why the guns had not blown a sitting, and unsuspecting target, right out of the sky!

The Hawkinge flight of Spitfires, not a full squadron you must remember, were now becoming a thorn in the Luftwaffe's sides. It was not that they were always prying into things on the other side of the Channel, but that each pilot was eager to cross swords with the enemy. They scrambled on any pretext whatsoever.

On December 5th, the airfield was attacked by three Bf 109s who had sneaked in under the radar screen. No warning had been given when the bomb-carrying fighters swept in from the West. One peculiar aspect of this small raid, which was to become a feature of future raids, was that as soon as the bombs were released the fighter-bombers went their different ways thus confusing the gunners. A more important factor which had obviously been overlooked was that the Luftwaffe unit had discovered a comparatively safe area through which they could enter and leave our coastline. It was some months before the gap in our defences was spotted and closed.

Two days later Sgt Gillies, flying the blue-painted Spitfire, returning from a reconnaissance patrol, saw a Dornier leaving the coast near Deal. He became so engrossed in shooting bits from it that he failed to notice that he was running out of fuel. Gillies managed to glide back by the skin of his teeth putting the aircraft into a nearby field just one mile from the aerodrome.

Sgt McKay found a JU88 having a field-day shooting up various installations at Dungeness ten days later. McKay gave it a five second burst and watched the raider zoom upwards shedding debris until, in the vertical, it suddenly dropped its nose and dived into the sea. he circled the area but saw no survivors.

Flt Lt Drake and Sgt Gillies on 19th noticed a Dornier with unusual markings flying at about 8,000 feet south of Dover. Fearing it might pull away and escape they made beam attacks and were startled to see a Very-Light cartridge shoot out from their intended victim. It was obvious the crew had mistaken the Spitfires for Messerschmitts loosing off the signal of the day. This mistake in aircraft recognition cost the German crew their lives. Flt Lt Drake celerated his new DFC at a party given at 'Bobby's' restaurant in Folkestone, with Sgt Don McKay receiving the toast for his DFM.

What an impressive record the Flight had achieved so far. The Spitfires were being patched up and repaired after dodgy landings and combat damage and only Sgt M. A. Lee had been lost when he failed to survive a crash-landing at Biggin Hill in poor visibility.

The Royal Air Force were now preparing to take the initiative and one of the last sorties performed by 421 Flight was as observers whilst Blenheims of 114 squadron, escorted by no less than six fighter squadrons, attacked shipping and ports in the Pas de Calais.

Airmen were discussing the rumour of the Flight being expanded to squadron strength when another three Bf 109 fighter-bombers damaged turf and proved more of a nuisance than a danger. Airmen were becoming so used to this type of attack that they stood and watched. The only airmen to move smartly were those reckoned to be in the raiders' path of attack.

The rumour came to fruition the following day. The Flight had been in action almost continuously since its inception just three months before. They had carried out no less than 199 patrols, destroying ten enemy aircraft, damaging nine more and claiming four 'probables'. This was no mean feat for a handful of pilots.

They were now to be known as No 91 (Nigerian) squadron and were destined to become one of the most professional fighter/reconnaissance units in Fighter Command, better known as the 'Jim Crow' squadron. This was largely due to the pilots who had developed their own system of navigation and their incredible audacity in attacking the enemy at close quarters in every conceivable situation.

The squadron was soon in the 'limelight' when Flt Lt 'Billy' Drake made headlines in the national press and got a mention in the BBC news bulletins. Billy had been at about 30,000 feet over northern France on a routine reconnaissnce sortie when his engine suddenly stopped. He was about seventy miles from Hawkinge and in an area infested with German fighters. 'If Sgt Gillies could do it then so can I', thought Billy. The flying control personnel had received his message and could only bite their finger nails with apprehension as he came gliding in over the Channel to make a perfect touchdown on the airfield. Others had tried the same feat with varying success. Some had lost their lives in the attempt. Plt Off Beake was at a very low altitude when the same thing happened on the same day. Beake put the Spitfire into a field at West Cut Farm and was injured and joined O'Meara in the Medical Inspection Room. O'Meara had crashed his Spitfire on the airfield when the brakes failed. Sqdn Ldr A. G. Malan, O.C., of No 74 squadron was just leaving the doctors' surgery when the other two arrived. Malan had put his ailing Spitfire down on the airfield with a glycol leak.

Two days later eight Spitfires of No 91 squadron were lined up on the tarmac at lunchtime. With cockpit canopies open and pilot harness laid out they stood like ballerinas off stage waiting for the prompter's call. Airmen fussed around them putting the finishing touches to the new squadron code

This fine picture taken by a Fox photographer shows 'Titch' Mynard refuelling the Spitfire Vb (DL–J—W3122), flown by the C.O. Sqdn Ldr Demozay, of No 91 (Nigerian) squadron in 1941. Just a few weeks before this photograph was taken 'Titch' was strafed by low—flying Messerschmitts whilst carrying out a similar task at A Flight dispersal.   (Fox Photos)

lettering and, one in particular, 'M' for Mike, was having another small white swastika painted under the cockpit.

A pale sun tried desperately to penetrate low cloud which, here and there, revealed large areas of blue. As each cloud passed over the airfield blotting out the blue sky its dark shadow seemed inseperable from the keen February wind. The Tannoy speakers suddenly crackled a curt message, 'Take Cover!'

Charles Mynard, a rigger, who had only arrived on the squadron the day previous, watched in utter astonishment as nine Bf 109s with guns blazing, hurtled over the trees near Terlingham Farm.

Nicknamed 'Titch', onle five feet two inches in his socks, he was perched on a wing-root of one of the Spitfires. His legs would not move. Hands white at the knuckles grasped the perspex windshield. He watched the bullets and cannon shells striking the grass tufts and creeping towards him. Someone was shouting at him to take cover. Then the bullets were striking the tarmac around him. Small holes appeared in the wing he was standing on. Bombs were exploding and the shrapnel whistled and whined. His ears were buzzing and became numb. An expressionless German face stared out at him as the nearest fighter-bomber sped over the hangar roofs. The roar of aero engines died away. The Bofors guns were still firing until they lost sight of the raiders.

He heard someone shouting his name. "Titch! Titch! — for Christ's sake, man!" He turned towards the voice. What he saw was so incredulous that he wanted to laugh. But somehow he couldn't. The voice was that of an airman who had dived into a large steel oil drum head first. A pair of black plimsolls waving in the air was the only tangible evidence that a body was there.

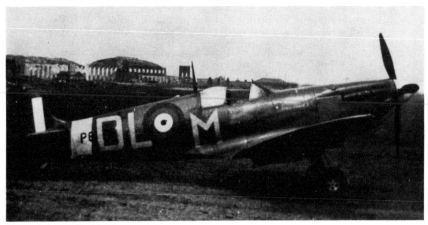

The Spitfire IIa in this picture was the mount usually flown by Sgt McKay, of No 91 (Nigerian) squadron. In the background can be seen damaged hangars, soon to be demolished.

(McKay collection)

There was an uncannny silence which followed then all hell broke loose. Some pilots were running towards their machines. Airmen suddenly appeared from the most unlikely places imaginable when the Bofors guns opened up again. The Messerschmitts had returned. A Spitfire's fuel tank exploded. It rocked on its wheels as it took the full blast and burst into flames. Sgt McKay stopped in his tracks and watched his aircraft 'M' for Mike, the little swastikas and the name 'Fairwarp', peeling off in the intense heat. It was soon a smouldering wreck.

For reasons best known to themselves the German JG26 unit pilots favoured these mid-day attacks and their ideas seemed to spread to other fighter units. It was on 8th February that two Bf 109s of II Schlageter LG2, made their lunchtime nuisance attack. One of them, a red-nosed Messerschmitt piloted by Werner Schlather, strafed Spitfires standing at their dispersal. Two were damaged. Only one bomb was dropped which exploded harmlessly on the field.

Schlather was wheeling about in the sky demonstrating great skill in manoeuvrability. It was like watching an aerobatic display, until he climbed into a loop immediately over the centre of the airfield. This attempt, a brash, almost over-confident gesture demonstrating an open defiance of the airfield defences, became his fatal mistake. As the aircraft flipped over into a dive the port wing crumpled under the blast from a Bofors shell. The undercarriage dropped down indicating that the hydraulics had been damaged and in a matter of seconds the fighter stalled. It lost height rapidly and screamed into a field near Arpinge Farm.

In the cemetery adjacent to the aerodrome, standing among others, is a tombstone simply inscribed 'Werner Schlather'. His body, together with the

Lt Werner Schlather of JI Lehrgeschwader LGII, shot down on February 8th 1941, by the Hawkinge gunners. Operating from Calais–Marck airfield on the French coast, Schlather's Bf 109 fighter dived into a field near the airfield where the pilot's body was found.
(Brenzett Aeronautical Museum)

remains of the fighter were found by Hawkinge personnel twelve feet below ground.

The changeover to Mark V Spitfires was more than welcome by the pilots of No 91 for, although earlier machines had served them well, certain modifications were desirable if the Spitfire was to remain a first class fighter able to compete with the latest German machines. Among many faults pilot discomfort at high altitudes was always a problem especially when climbing to reach a ceiling height of over 30,000 feet. A number of annoying faults were confined to the cockpit but others presented themselves. The carburettor for example had always been unreliable, failing completely when the aircraft was spun over onto its back during combat. At that kind of height the Spitfire was notoriously sluggish and required careful handling to keep the nose up. When diving from that altitude the perspex cockpit canopy would mist up. Sometimes the fuel gauge would ice up which, in a fighter of such short duration caused many accidents. Combined, these factors presented a major disadvantage in the face of superior German aircraft. These early deficiencies were overcome by the new technical developments embodied in the Mark V.

The fifteen Spitfire Mark Vs alloted to the squadron were considered to be donated by Nigeria and, as was the usual practice with 'presentation' aircraft, all were given names corresponding with a province in the donating country: Warri — Plateau — Ilorin — Kano — Abeokuta — Katsina — Niger — Oyo — Benin — Bornu — Cameroons — Calabar — Ijebu — Lagos Colony — Zaria and Onittsha.

With an increase in the rate of fire of the Browning machine guns, together with the punch of the Hispano cannons which had a higher muzzle

Grouped round Spitfire Vb — DL–H, of No 91 (Nigerian) squadron are left to right:—A. G. Donahue (American) – R. M. D. Hall – A. C. Younge (American) – Ronny Ingram – 'Polly' Perkins – Johnny Downs – 'Shag' O'Shaugnessy.   (Imperial War Museum)

velocity than the former, giving increased range with less deflection, the Mark Vs became a formidable weapon.

The squadron suffered its first casualty with their new aircraft a week later when, despite the use of 'Goose-neck' flares to assist landing in poor visibility, Plt Off P. McD. Hartas flew his Spitfire into the North Downs.

Pilots of the 'Jim Crow' squadron were predominantly of foreign origin such as French, Belgian, Dutch and Norwegian, although at one stage there were two Americans, a Canadian and two New Zealanders. Over five Flight Lieutenants were in the unit discounting the two Flight Commanders who of course, had certain administrative duties to perform; although this was nominal and involved little in contrast to those of the remainder of the squadron.

Primarily, now that the Luftwaffe had reduced their large formation sorties, the reconnaissance work was concerned with enemy shipping which, while within the close confines of the English Channel, held high regard for the effectiveness of the RAF. As a direct result only a few, if any, German ships left harbour during the daylight hours. In ports they relied for protection upon the deadly flak defences which were found to be notoriously accurate. When they had to move they usually did so in convoy and if this was in any way impracticable they had an escort of flak ships to ward off aerial attacks.

Reconnaissance areas covered by the 'Jim Crows' ranged from Le Havre in the west to the Hague in the east and, between these two extremities, lay the harbours of Fecamp, Dieppe, Le Treport, the Somme Estuary,

Boulogne, Calais, Gravelines, Dunkirk, Nieuport, Ostende, Zeebrugge, Blankenburg and Flushing. Enemy shipping were forced to find sanctuary during daylight at any one of these ports otherwise they would be spotted. Hence the Hawkinge squadron operated dawn and dusk patrols which were the most likely times to discover shipping outside harbours. When spotted the anti-shipping Hurri-bombers would be alerted to make their strike, providing the intelligence sections were able to deduce from pilots' reports whether an attack was worthwhile.

Although reconnaisance sorties would usually go from Dieppe to Cap Gris Nez on the westward route and from Ostend to Cap Gris Nez on the eastward route, the tactical way in which a particular 'recce' was carried out was solely that of the pilot concerned and each devised his own method. It is perhaps significant that no two pilots seemed ever to perform a 'recce' in a similar way and, what is more surprising, individual preferences for flying high, or choosing to hug the sea, were never consistent. They constantly changed their tactics, inviting our own coastal defences to fire at them before identification. More than one 'Jim Crow' pilot was to pay the supreme penalty for exercising his own individuality. However, equally important was that the enemy were never certain where the routine 'recces' would come from.

Squadron casualties were surprisingly light in view of the regularity with which 'recce' patrols were carried out, and their quota of 'kills' and 'probables' mounted steadily. In April there had been about ten crashes to contend with. Fortunately most crashed machines had been repairable. Sgt McKay got his twelfth 'kill' on 6th March, but later that month he was extremely lucky to get back at all from an intercepted patrol over Calais. Sgt Spears and Mann at 7,000 feet over Dover were suddenly confronted with a pack of Messerschmitts. Travelling in an easterly direction they both climbed for cover in cloud over St Margaret's Bay. Spears was forced to bail out over Little Mongeham. Mann fought a losing battle and steered for Hawkinge with his engine alight. Suffering burns to hands and face he managed to get the aircraft down near Paddlesworth in a belly-flop.

There were three airmen casualties on 10th March when a Bf 109 dropped a well-aimed bomb close to 'B' Flight dispersal about 17.00 hrs. The raider was soon out of sight sideslipping round Sugar-Loaf hill and out over Folkestone before the gunners were aware of what had happened. Sqdn Ldr Henneburg and Sgt Popek, both of No 303 (Polish) squadron, met the raider going out as they were coming in with fuel tanks reading empty. Both Spitfires ran on to soft mud and up-ended in an area shunned by the resident squadron.

High explosive bombs straddled nearby fields which aroused only slight interest from slumbering airmen at 02.30 hrs on a perfect moonlit night of 14th March. Airmen were becoming complacent.

It was very nearly 15.45 hrs on 12th April, when excited messages were received from pilots of No 303 (Polish) squadron, who were returning from a sweep over Northern France. They had received a formidable pounding from the German flak defences on the coast. Their C.O., Henneberg, was last seen diving towards the sea. Six Spitfires of the squadron remained over the area in the hope that Henneberg would be sighted in his dinghy. Low on fuel those six Spitfires were now heading for Hawkinge, having been relieved by the Hurricanes of No 302 (Polish) squadron. Thirty minutes later the refuelled Spitfires were taking off for their base at Northolt. The Hurricanes were the next to run low on fuel and arrived at the airfield from different directions. They all began to approach and make their landings at the same time. Flying Control personnel were frantic in their efforts to warn the Polish pilots by radio but to no avail. Red Very-Lights shot up into the sky like fireworks. Two of the Hurricanes landed side by side in the middle of the airfield and, running out of grass, they both tipped up on their spinners near the fuel dump. Another came in from the south, veered round to face west and careered into a parked Spitfire of the resident squadron at 'A' Flight dispersal. The fourth Hurricane, at exactly the same moment, belly-flopped in the opposite direction coming to rest near the remains of No 3 hangar. Airmen could only stand and wonder at the shambles. They had never experienced anything like it.

Sgt McKay was in trouble again when over Cap Gris Nez. He had just claimed his thirteenth 'kill' but not without sustaining heavy damage. With a cockpit canopy shattered into a basket weave effect he wound his seat up to its fullest extent and, with the hood right back settled down to open cockpit flying. He can be forgiven for an error of judgement some weeks later when he forgot to lower his undercarriage whilst landing. But an airman attempting to warn the luckless pilot with a red Very-Light, fell over in haste and the fizzing cartridge disappeared into a bell tent. The occupants, certain they were under attack, vacated the tent smartly!

Conscious of the limited success rate in identifying sneak raiders the Station Wing Commander put out airmen on strategically placed positions on high ground linked to Flying Control by landline. These mostly unannounced strafing raids were usually at midday which was responsible for a keen sense of awareness in airfield personnel. Reluctance to remain in the dining room longer than was absolutely necessary caused bouts of indigestion but aircraftsman Gordon Taylor thought it was a small price to pay for one's personal safety when two seperate strafing raids were made on 8th and 11th, causing utter confusion when airmen dived under dining tables.

On Friday 19th May, the airfield was attacked no less than four times on the one day. The first occasion was at 12.50 hrs when Wg Cmdr Fry, MC, the station C.O., was on the steps of the Officers' Mess talking to his distinguished visitor, Group Captain Beamish. Three yellow-nosed Messerschmitts had slipped in under the radar screen just as whistles were being blown. Bullets ripped into the Hispano gun-pits with deadly accuracy and the soldiers manning them were unable to return the fire. As the raiders disappeared over the village roofs the Tannoy clicked into life with 'Take Cover . . . Take Cover!'

A petrol bowser had arrived at 'B' Flight dispersal especially to refuel Beamish's Hurricane. Aircraftsman Taylor was standing on the wing root with the hoze nozzle in the petrol tank when the second strafing raid took place. With 100 octane fuel pumping through he was unable to move. Without so much as a tin helmet for protection he watched the bullets tearing towards the Hurricane. He could only flinch when they reached the port wing tip. The tracer bullets, white hot, sizzled through the air making cracking sounds to his ears.

Beamish's Hurricanes had just left the airfield when the Observer Corps post near Deal spotted a small formation of Messerschmitts swinging inland over the southern collieries. They were unsure of the target for tip-and-run raids usually ranged along the coast bombing and machine gunning towns and villages at random. All the available Spitfires of No 91 squadron were scrambled and vectored to a position over the Channel between St Margaret's and Folkestone at no more than 2,000 feet.

At about 14.30 hrs, in line abreast, four Messerschmitts were skimming the treetops at Reindene Wood to the north of the village. The inevitable bullets and cannon shells preceded their headlong rush over the airfield at no more than 100 feet. But there were no aircraft sitting waiting to be shot up. The Bofors put up a fierce barrage traversing with the raiders until they were out of sight. The PAC rockets, set off too late to be effective, swished into an empty sky. Out over the Channel 91 squadron pounced upon their quarry disposing of two Bf 109s in as many seconds. Only one of the enemy fighters managed to reach its French base. One airman had been killed and five others injured in the flying debris. Some airmen, seeing the PAC rocket parachutes descending were convinced they were parachutists. But, as one remarked years later, "In the event of an invasion we were supposed to be fully equipped to deal with it. Our anti-para outfit consisted of a tin hat, a pair of gumboots, a respirator and a pickaxe handle with a sharpened piece of metal railing stuck in the end. I never saw a rifle during the whole of 1941!"

The next attack was made in the evening at 19.00 hrs and consisted of a much larger force of fighter-bombers in waves of three. A similar raid was being made on Lympne at the same time and both were using the new Bf 109F which had entered service with the Luftwaffe in January. Fortunately the raid had been logged by radar enabling the 'Jim Crow' squadron to get up before the enemy arrived. What might have been a severe attack was thwarted by the sheer weight of anti-aircraft shells which plastered the evening sky in one huge barrier of defence. Bombs were dropped across the whole of the airfield causing extensive damage to buildings especially in the dispersal areas. Bell tents were riddled with holes and empty ammunition boxes flew into the air. Behind the tents were two dustbins full to the brim with 100 octane petrol, an unofficial fuelling point for a light grey Flying Standard 12 and a Chrysler 'Airflow'. Neither motor-car was damaged but the dustbins were holed. Although helped by low cloud the raiders made good their escape by hugging the sea but two were brought down by the resident squadron.

That night Canterbury received a heavy raid at 22.00 hrs and it was from this direction that two bombers arrived over the airfield releasing their high explosives. Two air raid shelters were blown up and the temporary roof of No 2 hangar caved in upon a couple of Spitfires and the C.O.'s Magister.

The following day No 2 hangar was declared utterly useless and was ordered to be demolished. Airmen and soldiers worked side by side to clear up the mess while gunners scanned the horizon for fear of another attack.

By now the RAF fighter squadrons had begun to take the initiative and to some extent gain a foothold in air superiority. Wing leaders, and squadron leaders, scouring the French coasts looking for trouble, often shot up German held air-fields in an attempt to stir up the inevitable hornets' nest. It was on returning from one of these sweeps over France that a Spitfire of No 616 squadron, flown by Flt Lt Dundas, nearly put paid to a number of Hawkinge Spitfires. With Sqdn Ldr Bader watching his descent, Dundas put his ailing aircraft down beside the lined-up aircraft. 'Paddy' Green, the C.O. nearly had a fit as he watched the slithering machine belly-flop near his squadron. 'Cocky' Dundas, having disentangled himself from the bent cockpit, was immediately subject to some well chosen expletives. Greens' concern was heightened because he had just received a signal to have his squadron ready to fly at strength escorting Blenheims over French ports. A confident squadron of Spitfires arrived over the French port of Dunkirk amidst flak bursts at the right height and at the right time, but no bombers. The Blenheims had gone to the wrong Dunkirk and were circling the radar towers near Canterbury!

The number of airmen at Hawkinge was becoming a problem, for accommodation was at a premium. Until the training machine was geared to receive the hundreds of waiting airmen destined for aircrew, they were, unfortunately farmed out to various RAF stations to make themselves useful. Hawkinge amongst others was selected although no one could understand why. There were quieter aerodromes in the British Isles. These luckless airmen were supposed to be given a certain amount of instruction in aeronautical subjects but, initially, were often used to good effect in the cookhouse, scouring saucepans and everything else associated with cooking. The more senior of these disillusioned airmen were, however, elevated to machine gunners on the defensive posts around the airfield periphery. No specific training was given in handling weapons and it is little wonder that, although they were keen to blaze away when the airfield was under attack, they failed to hit anything!

Most of them were billetted in accommodation which had received severe damage and were obliged to bathe and shower and attend to their more private functions in the open. Plumbing and fittings had been smashed, walls and ceilings had vanished completely. Moving to the main barrack blocks proved to be of no advantage, for these had not escaped damage either. It was not unusual to find snowdrifts down the centre of the barrack room since most of the roof had disappeared. Glass was a luxury as most windows were boarded up. Walls cracked by bomb blast let in rain. The station HQ had been bombed out three times. The wireless section had nowhere to store their delicate equipment. Other stores vital to an operational squadron was often heaped together under tarpaulins. Most of these serviceable items were in danger of being blown up, damaged by blast or ruined by dampness.

To reduce this concentration of valuable airmen and equipment various sections were dispersed away from the now dilapidated aerodrome. Private houses in and around the village were taken over as were large manor-type houses further afield such as Hockley Soul in the Alkham Valley. The swimming pool at White Gates near Swingfield was a pleasurable amenity not to be missed. The HQ section eventually enjoyed the luxury of a half-timbered cottage known as Maypole Farm.

In the course of time, those in authority realised that something should be done about educating the aircrew trainees. But they failed to consider the possible consequences of permanent curvature of the spine when assigning the group to the village school. The desks had been designed for little people. But it was here they were lectured on aeronautical subjects by an effete young fighter pilot who had been wounded in a dogfight but who was a hero to his students!

With the increased activity of offensive sweeps, damaged aircraft made for Hawkinge and would suddenly appear through swirling mists and fog, at very low altitude and guided between treetops by nervous jerking rudders. Some were so damaged by German flak batteries that they were no longer airworthy. Catastrophic events were daily occurrences and the ambulance and crash tender were in great demand. It was reminiscent of the previous summer.

There were a number of changes in 91 squadron personnel. The American Plt Off A. G. Donahue, who had seen action in 1940, volunteered for the Far East. Contemporary reports suggested he wanted more action! Flying his Spitfire named 'Message of Minnesota', he had achieved two 'kills' with the 'Jim Crow' unit and, as a Flight Commander with No 258 squadron flew Hurricanes in the defence of Ceylon and was one of the last to leave Singapore. Flt Lt R. A. Lee-Knight, DFC, who had been shot down only a month before also left the squadron with a score of three Bf 109s to his credit. He was later killed defending Malta. Joining the squadron was Flt Lt Jean Demozay, a Free French pilot had escaped from his country and flew in

Jean Demozay the Free French pilot of No 91 (Nigerian) squadron, who flew under the name of Moses Morlaix and was awarded DSC, DFC and Bar, CL, CG with nine Palms, had a record of 21 victories.
(Imperial War Museum)

The American Sergeant Pilot A. C. Younge of Cleveland U.S.A. with his Spitfire Vb of No 91 (Nigerian) squadron at Hawkinge 1941. (Imperial War Museum)

exile as 'Moses Morlaix'. Dark, suave and neat of appearance, Moses was more of an introvert than others of his own nationality. Self-disciplined, confident and completely independent he was a fine fighter pilot. Sqdn Ldr Watts-Farmer, DFC, took over the unit from 'Paddy' Green at a time of tremendous pride in squadron achievements.

The ground crews were as enthusiastic as the pilots. Combat reports were discussed well into the night and there existed great rivalry between the 'A' and 'B' Flights. Aircraft were fussed over into the late hours, cleaned and polished, patched and repaired and woe betide any pilot who had forgotten to activate the camera-gun button. Even a system of fines was introduced by the ground crew. Leaving the flaps in the 'locked-down' position cost the pilot two shillings and sixpence — it was five shillings if the gun-button safety catch was left in the 'OFF' position. It cost Sgt Plt Sykes six pints of beer when he returned with damaged propeller tips, caused by flying too low over the Channel! There existed also a bond of friendship between some pilots and their ground crew. One pilot in particular was sometimes brought back to camp, especially if he was to be on the 'Dawn Patrol' next morning, and put to bed with a hot drink!

CHAPTER TEN
Seascape, August 1941–August 1942

Before 1940 our air sea rescue service was practically non-existent and during the air battles of that summer rescue operations at sea relied on the Royal Navy and the Lifeboat Service. The RAF were in possession of a number of high speed launches which were based at selected coastal stations around the country but were only responsible for the location of airmen in distress. But within a year, as operations over the Continent increased, it was essential for the RAF to have its own rescue service completely independent of the Navy. Fighter Command borrowed a small number of Lysander aircraft from the Army Co-operation squadrons. With four rubber dinghies attached to the wheel carriers they were a most welcome sight to a ditched airman. Although the Lysanders carried twin Browning machine guns they were, nevertheless, considered easy prey for prowling enemy fighters, and so a pair of escorting Spitfires were allocated for their protection. In 1940 rescue from the sea was a matter of urgency as fighter pilots especially had not yet been provided with a rubber dinghy.

The first air sea rescue Lysander to operate from Hawkinge was borrowed from 'B' Flight No 4 Army Co-operation squadron then at Manston and began in December 1940. Nearly a year was to elapse before the Flight was replaced by a full operational rescue unit when in June 1941, 'A' Flight No 277 (ASR) squadron was formed. A month later they received two Walrus amphibians, the single-engined, three-seater pusher type biplane designed in the early 1930s for fleet spotter work.

The 'Wally', 'Shagbat' or 'Steam Pigeon', nicknames remembered with nostalgia by many, was a robustly constructed aircraft which received much affection from pilots and crew. The record of the air sea rescue squadron at the airfield is quite remarkable. It is a record of courage and endurance and shows the commendable sense of responsibility for saving human life. In the most appalling weather conditions one can ever imagine these few men flew thousands of miles over the English Channel and North Sea, searching hour after hour for a minute shape on the grey wastes.

Because of the RAF increased bomber and fighter operations the Luftwaffe were now finding difficulty in maintaining adequate defence. As a direct result additional fighter pilots were posted to the French based units from the Eastern Front. Records show that RAF fighter losses, both pilots and aircraft, rose at an alarming rate. The 'Jim Crow' squadron for example, a comparatively small unit, lost over ten pilots up to December of that year. Plt Off Gage just disappeared, then Sgt Thornbur failed to return from his recce. Sgt Baker and Plt Off Warden were both shot down whilst orbiting an

The unofficial insignia of No 277 (ASR) squadron, originally painted in colour on the walls of the crew room at Hawkinge. 1942. (D. Hartwell)

The only known photograph of the first Lysander borrowed from No 4 (AC) squadron and subsequently used on air sea rescue duties at Hawkinge with Hurricane escort.

(D. Hartwell)

Flt Lt J. J. Le Roux, DFC, a South African pilot of No 91 (Nigerian) squadron showing his Springbok emblem on the Mae West. Le Roux was later credited with shooting-up the German staff car belonging to Rommel. (Imperial War Museum)

air sea rescue launch. The South African pilot Chris Le Roux increased his personal score by shooting down two Bf 109s. Five days later he was shooting up a German airfield at Burck-Sur-Mer, leaving in his wake damaged Messerschmitts, a petrol bowser and, of all things, a fire engine! Sgt 'Olly' Cooper, Le Roux's wingman, was last seen diving into the sea in poor visibility.

Plt Off Andrews was fed up with telling Group that the German airfield at St Valery-En-Caux, WAS operational and not a dummy as they had suggested. To prove his point he paid the airfield a visit. He attacked at very low level raking everything in sight with his cannons then, whilst the Germans were running about, Andrews calmly flew back at reduced speed and photographed the scene. Fighter Command were impressed to say the least!

Flt Sgt Doug Hartwell and Sgt Jones of No 277 (ASR) squadron had rather a lucky escape on 27th October. They had cleared dispersal in four minutes after receiving the scramble message that there was a 'customer' for them some fifteen miles south of Dover. Reaching the area Hartwell began the long and laborious figure of eight manoeuvre over the sea where insignificant shapes could conjure themselves into objects requiring further investigation at low level. A pale, watery sun was hidden behind a mass of woolly cloud producing large dark shadows upon the sea making it infinitely more difficult to spot their 'customer'.

Sgt Jones had long since removed the safety catches on his twin Brownings to the OFF position and, was peering over the side of the fuselage when a hail of bullets ripped along the starboard side. The Sgt gunner, who had only fired his guns in practice, let alone being fired at himself, looked up to see red tracer curving towards him sparkling against the back-cloth of white cloud. He swung the Brownings round until the small outline of a Messerschmitt filled his sights. He just managed to squeeze the triggers when Hartwell threw the Lysander to port and down. Throttle wide open the Mercury engine roared its protest as it dived towards the sea. Jones hung on grimly and could only fire his guns when the Lysander levelled out. A wavering image filled his sights and he squeezed. He watched one of the three assailants sheer off as bits flew from it. Then the two escorting Spitfires arrived. It was a sight that Jones and Hartwell will never forget.

Almost at sea level Hartwell turned for home. He could see large areas of sky through the wings. Oil splashed through the shattered windshield and covered his face. He struggled to keep the ailing Lysander on an even keel. The fifteen minutes to reach the North Downs above Folkestone seemed more like fifteen hours. They limped over the perimeter fence and then the Lysander touched down. Hartwell let it roll towards the centre of the airfield. When the machine stopped he switched off the engine. Only the crackles of the cooling exhaust stubs invaded their innermost thoughts.

The Engineering Officer had his biggest job yet when a Wellington of No 12 squadron crash landed in a field nearby. A few days later a dozen Spitfires and a handful of Hurricanes came in to refuel, then another two Wellingtons with Tomahawks as escort, and over twenty Blenheims arrived to take part in Army manoeuvres. One of them crashed with a faulty undercarriage.

On an extremely cold, blustery day, troops made a mock attack on the aerodrome through driving snow squalls. According to the umpire's report the RAF were wiped out to a man!

The three German battleships, Scharnhorst, Gneisenau and Prinz Eugen left their moorings in Brest harbour just after 22.00 hrs on 11th February 1942, to run the gauntlet of the English Channel. At dawn the following day the German fighter ace Adolf Galland sent up his first fighters to relieve the night cover which had flown protection patrols continuously over this formidable armada. At almost the same time the two Spitfires on dawn patrol left their dispersal at Hawkinge. Out in the middle of the Channel the two aircraft parted company one flying towards Ostend, the other turning right towards Le Havre. On their return both pilots reported some 'E' Boat activity in various harbours although no significnce was attached to this. A second pair of Spitfires flew out over the Channel at 10.20 hrs. Sqdn Ldr 'Bobby' Oxspring with Sgt Beaumont as his wingman, were flying over the German battleships some ten minutes later.

Visbility was fairly reasonable although some rain clouds were building up over the French coast. But there was no mistaking the importance of what they had stumbled on. Oxspring called up the sector controller and informed him of the three battleships and seven escorting destroyers. Normally radio silence was strictly observed by the 'Jim Crow' pilots. Nevertheless, this particular radio message was monitored by the Germans and Galland's fighters were alerted. Meanwhile Oxspring and Beaumont flew back to base at full throttle. Their sighting was later confirmed by another pair of Spitfires who had flown over the same area on an unofficial joy ride.

The RAF began to organise their attacking force. Six Swordfish torpedo-carrying aircraft of the Fleet Air Arm flew out from nearby Manston in the face of Hell itself. The result was suicidal for all were lost in what was described as one of the most courageous exploits ever flown by the FAA.

No 91 squadron played but a small part in that infamous engagement on 12th February. They continued with their lone recce sorties calmly and methodically shooting up harbour installations, shipping, gun positions and radar sites when the opportunity arose.

Fighter and Bomber Command operations grew in number and with more squadrons flying as wings it became a complex business for controllers at sector. Gone were the days when squadrons operated singly and now every sortie was planned down to the last detail. Even the type of aircraft had changed causing even more confusion. Our own aircraft were accidentally being shot at in increasing numbers. It was inevitable. New and quite unfamiliar types were being used in the light-bombing attacks. As fast as our Hawker Typhoons and twin-engined Mosquitoes came off the production lines they went into operation. The new Hurricanes and the latest Spitfire with new-fangled attachments looked odd and were approached with suspicion. In addition we were using the American Bostons, Havoc, Marylands, Mitchells and Baltimores, which were all light bombers with a good turn of speed. The American fighters, such as the Thunderbolts and Mustangs, added to the confusion and were shot at by our own fighters and gunners!

Tremendous seas and gale force winds caused havoc among the shipping lanes when mines broke free from their moorings. Doug Hartwell got his machine off the grass and climbed out towards Swingfield on the evening of 16th April, for a late mine-spotting patrol in the Dover area. But the patrol ended rather rapidly when the Lysander developed engine trouble over Reindene Wood. The big Mercury engine coughed and stopped turning. Hartwell 'blipped' the switches quickly in the faint hope the engine would splutter into life. He had experienced a similar dilemma with a jammed throttle control twelve days earlier. Usually engine failure in a Lysander presented little difficulty. The high wing of the machine afforded plenty of lift and the aircraft required little forward speed to enable the pilot to get down, providing that height was sufficient to clear obstacles. Hartwell could not have been in a worse position — over a wooded area. He could see a field the other side of the wood but his speed was dropping off rapidly and he

The wreckage of Sgt Hartwell's Lysander which developed an engine fault over Reindene Wood. The gunner Gordon Jones, never flew again for he had suffered head injuries. (D. Hartwell)

was no more than three hundred feet up. The undercarriage caught the trees bringing the nose of the aircraft down. The Lysander cartwheeled. The massive radial engine had, on impact, thrust back into the cockpit pinning Hartwell to his seat. But somehow he managd to claw his way through the twisted metal to find Sgt Jones entangled, unconscious and seriously injured. Jones never flew again.

It was in April that Sqdn Ldr Oxspring made the first night sortie over France in good moonlight and excellent visibility. On another clear moonlit night a month later Flt Lt Silk with Plt Off Maridor as wingman made squadron history by carrying out the first offensive night patrol over occupied France. Silk flew down the Somme Estuary then turned towards Dieppe and along the coast to Cap Gris Nez. They attacked four coasters and returned at 02.20 hrs.

A few days later Maridor, a Frenchman, made a terrible mistake in aircraft recognition. He was returning from patrol near St Margaret's Bay, when he spotted what he thought were two Messerschmitts on a reciprocal course. At the first sign of Maridor's tracers passing their aircraft the two Canadians broke right and left. The Frenchman dived between them and then discovered his error, but it was too late. Both Spitfires returned fire whilst Maridor was climbing above the cliffs. Maridor set course for Hawkinge with the two disgruntled Canadians in hot pursuit. Without waiting to receive clearance to land, the Frenchman touched down but, due to a punctured tyre, the Spitfire flipped over onto its back. While he was being disentangled from the cockpit the two Canadians vented their tempers in vitriolic language.

From about mid-1942 onwards the heavy daylight raids made by the American 8th and 9th air forces on German industrial targets caused a constant stream of damaged B17 Fortresses and Liberators, on various headings, heights and speeds, to crashing either in the Channel or on land adjacent to the coast.

A Boulton-Paul Defiant of No 277 (Air Sea Rescue) squadron. Squadron code BA–A was in red. (D. Hartwell)

Pressure on our existing air sea rescue squadrons influenced the Air Ministry to review the much-maligned Boulton—Paul Defiant. By February 1942 trials began to test its ASR suitability and three months later No 277 (ASR) squadron received six to supplement the four Lysanders already on strength. Modifications to the Defiant's wings were made at squadron level to accommodate the 'M8 type dinghy. It turned out to be the first disadvantage because only one such dinghy could be carried under each wing compared to the four carried by the Lysander. However, the increased strength of the squadron was a valuable asset when the unit operated from Shoreham during the Dieppe raid in August of that year. But just six months after their introduction it was evident that the Defiant was not at all suitable. For one thing they were taking up valuable time in engine overhauls and hangar space was at a premium since only one survived the bombing raids, and only one blister hangar had been erected by then.

Pilots were disillusioned with the Defiant's performance. A rather high stalling speed and wide turning arc, both important factors in ASR work, were an insufferable imposition. Once again the Defiant, whose role in service with various RAF commands, had proved considerably less than spectacular, gradually disappeared from air sea rescue squadrons leaving the Lysander supreme until the arrival of the ASR Spitfire.

By the autumn No 91 squadron's radius of action had increased and stretched to its limits, they were fequently called upon to fly as far east as the Zuider Zee and Le Havre in the west. There was no room for navigational

151

Fitting the dinghies to a Lysander of No 277 (Air Sea Rescue) squadron at Hawkinge in 1942.
(Kent Messenger)

errors for they carried no auxiliary fuel tanks. The normal supply was only just adequate. The recce patrols were still being made at regular times, unaltered from the squadron's inception and, without exception, the dawn and dusk sorties were regulated almost by the clock. The Intelligence Officer, however, had often been heard to make the remark, 'Why doesn't Gerry intercept our chaps more often?' They found the answer when a German pilot called Peter Kruger, flying the latest Focke Wulf 190 fighter, was shot down by members of the squadron and visited in Victoria Hospital, Dover soon afterwards. He told that it was not for the want of trying that they seldom encountered the 'Jim Crow' squadron patrols. But they found difficulty in foreseeing the direction and height at which the individual aircraft would appear. 91 squadron pilots were a little gratified at this if not flattered to hear that their own particular methods of flying patrols had so upset their opponents. Their opponents were mainly dispersed on the coastal airfields, Calais—Marck was one and Abbeville near the Somme estuary another. It was through Kruger they discovered that the unit based at Abbeville bore the name Manfred von Richtofen and was considered a crack fighter unit.

Newcomers to 91 squadron were to learn and perfect the art of shooting at all manner of targets on the French coast and those who were inclined towards the more excitable features of deliberate self-expression found bigger and better targets further inland. It was usually further inland that targets were found for the moonlight sorties such as aerodromes, rail and road traffic. The curfew imposed on the French population enabled the intruders to be almost positive that any targets attacked would be military. The obvious necessity of avoiding heavily defended areas was of paramount importance if the intruders were to return unscathed. Approaching the French coast at night was like entering the den of some prehistoric monster whose luminous tentacles stabbed out towards you. By diving and altering course it was possible to avoid the searchlights. The bomber was not so lucky.

Appalling weather conditions during the daylight hours grounded most other fighter squadrons but not the 'Jim Crow' squadron. Low level cloud and intermittent rain squalls became quite suitable for their special exploits although they sometimes got lost and had to rely on the two radio trucks 'Y' and 'Z' to talk them back to the airfield.

Flt Lt Geoff Pannell, a New Zealander, was returning from dawn patrol in a thick pea-souper. A huge watery sun was doing its utmost to disperse the heavy mists which, 2,000 feet below covered the sea completely in an undulating blanket of swirling white. It was tranquil moments like this which betrayed the fighter pilot's trained instinct and the unexplained disappearance of many of our aircraft to the malleability of the mind.

Pannell saw the dim outline of the coast rising out of the mists about three miles ahead. He changed course and flew along parallel with the cliffs following the contour round to Dover, where barrage balloons stuck out of the white virgin fog like sausages on sticks. He imagined the anti-aircraft guns traversing with the sound of his engine and was thankful that his Pip-squeak IFF was working.

Suddenly his headphones crackled into life. It was the sector controller informing him of a possible 'bandit' approaching Folkestone. More by luck than judgment Pannell suddenly found that he was immediately behind a Bf 109 practically on a reciprocal course. He flicked on his gun-sight and released the safety catch. The pale orange glow of the gun-sight enveloped the German fighter. The pilot seemed unaware he was being followed for he took no evasive action. Pannell held the aircraft steady and then gave a three-second burst. He watched the cannon shells slam into the Messerschmitt and, without altering course, he saw it gradually dip towards the blanket of fog and then it disappeared.

Another New Zealander had a similar experience although he was just beginning his patrol. Small and unimposing Flt Lt 'Spud' Spurdle was, at first appearance, unassuming but managed to conceal from strangers his natural humour and lively personality. Visibility was poor and it was raining quite heavily when he took off at dawn crossing the coast at Sandgate. There had been no warning of a possible 'bandit' in the vicinity and it is open to conjecture who was more surprised when both aircraft appeared on a collision course. Spurdle flicked up into a loop and came out of it, much to his surprise, not very far behind the Messerschmitt which had not altered course at all. Closing fast and in a shallow dive Spurdle pressed the gun button. The German machine climbed into cloud and Spurdle gave chase. They came out of cloud into bright sunlight at no more than 3,000 feet. The Bf 109 ahead was slowly turning over onto its back then slipped back into cloud. Spurdle lost sight of it and decided to drop through the cloud to sea level. Almost immediately he saw a body lying face down in the water wearing German green overalls and an unopened parachute. Although there were no signs of any wreckage there was no doubt in his mind that he had shot the 'bandit' down.

Flt Lt Andrews in the new Spitfire Mk VI, a high altitude variant with special pointed wing-tips and a pressurised cockpit, remained undetected whilst stalking a JU88 along the French coast. After making notes on the camouflage, unit insignia and armament, he calmly shot it down within sight of the Cap Gris Nez beach. On his return, however, he in turn was followed by one of the latest and most formidable of German fighters, the Focke Wulf 190. As luck would have it, Flt Lt Chris Le Roux, the South African who had joined the squadron the year previous, was returning from patrol. Le Roux saw the FW 190 about to make his attack on Andrews. Slightly behind and to port he gave the unsuspecting German a full three-second burst of 20 mm cannon shells. The FW 190 rolled over and hit the sea at terrific speed.

The Focke Wulf 190, using the radial engine combined with a slim fusel-age, was another of the successful fighters to be developed during the Second World War. It was superior to anything the RAF could muster until the Mk IX Spitfire and Hawker Typhoon came on the scene. The Mk V Spit-fire was the best fighter we had then but the FW 190 was still about twenty miles an hour faster and dived and turned with comparative ease.

Hawkinge became host to two fighter squadrons in June who were to oper-ate 'Sweeps' and 'Rhubarbs' from the airfield, with Spitfires fitted with wing drop-tanks. Selected targets further afield than was usual were now possible. Three additional corrugated blister hangars had been hastily erected to accommodate aircraft for servicing schedules. No 65 squadron was the first to arrive followed by No 41 squadron and both were operating with Spitfire Mk Vbs, but after just one month they were moved north pending their postings overseas.

After a delay of over a month Operation Jubilee (Dieppe Raid) was finally made on 19th August. Like other airfields in the south and east, Hawkinge became a stronghold with movements in and around the area curtailed to a minimum using passes. The night before the raid took place two Spitfire squadrons arrived, No 416 and No 616, the latter operating the Spitfire Mk VI for high cover over the landings.

At the end of October No 137 squadron, operating Whirlwinds from Manston, sent four to bomb a German camp at Etaples. Only one of them managed to get back. Flt Lt John Van Schaik nearly made it but had to ditch five miles out from the French coast. When the Hawkinge Walrus arrived in the area he was spotted paddling furiously towards England surrounded by mines. Despite his warnings the Walrus alighted and picked him up but there was some very tense moments trying to get the amphibian off. It is recorded that Schaik was put to bed at Hawkinge suffering from shock.

A kind of ultimate irony exists when a pilot who has perhaps, quite unwittingly, achieved outstanding success with a steady mounting score, is suddenly aware that he has become the conscience of the squadron. Fame can engulf his personality and in the end, he is required to maintain a frantic schedule as if it is expected of him. This frenetic pace took its toll when the American Art Donahue, recently posted back to 91 squadron after his escape from Singapore, craved the destruction of an elusive JU88 nightfighter. On a previously unsatisfactory encounter he had managed to set one engine alight. That particular combat proved inconclusive as intelligence reports later confirmed that the machine had actually landed in Belgium. The American was a determined character and left the airfield at a very early hour on 11th September. His trace on the radar screen, a mere bright blob, disappeared and operations rang through to ask for a special search to be undertaken in the Ostend area.

It was 'A' Flight's turn for the dawn patrol that morning which was usually about 05.00 hrs, but Roger Hall was roused from his slumbers at 04.30 hrs and, as he put it years later, "I was not a little uncritical of Art's stupidity!"

Flt Lt Roger Hall with the thoughts of Donahue sitting in the sea somewhere dispelled any angry feelings toward him, took off through the early morning mists still clinging to the ground. Arriving at a point just off Cap Gris Nez he found visibility rather poor and was obliged to come down to below 200 feet where the sea was hardly distinguishable! It was then that sector control called him up with a deteriorating weather report! Roger broke away sharply when the dark bulwarks of Dunkirk harbour suddenly loomed before him. He was in a typical pea-souper. One slip and he would be in danger of going to a watery grave. It was increasingly obvious that a search in these conditions was quite out of the question. Control gave him a course setting for home. Visibility at Hawkinge was down to one hundred yards. He leaned forwards intent on his instruments and listened to the course corrections made at intervals. The Spitfire was engulfed in a white shroud-like web and Roger could see nothing at all when, on the final course setting, he was told that the airfield should be beneath him. He reduced his height until he saw some aerodrome buildings and, carefully estimating his position, landed in the gloom. Art Donahue was never recovered.

The Luftwaffe 'hit-and-run' activities broadened towards the autumn of 1942, with one of the biggest daylight raids made by fighter-bombers since

155

Flt Lt R. M. D. Hall, DFC, of 'A' Flight No 91
(Nigerian) squadron.   (R. M. D. Hall)

the Battle of Britain. It was late one Saturday evening on 30th September that 91 squadron scrambled to intercept raiders in the vicinity of Canterbury. They came face to face with the enemy who were fleeing towards the Channel. The evening sky became alive with twisting, turning Spitfires and FW 190s. Both the C.O., Moses and Chris Le Roux destroyed two machines in as many minutes. But the German pilots stayed to fight. The C.O. returned to the airfield out of ammunition and was careering across the grass within eight minutes to rejoin the battle. Incredibly, he got another FW 190 when he shot it into the sea. Flt Sgt Gibbs was last seen chasing an enemy machine across the Channel. When 91 squadron returned some of them began performing victory rolls. The local controller counted them as best he could. Jubilant pilots were coaxed down for a landing, one by one, like naughty school boys. The Intelligence Officer credited the squadron with five kills and four damaged. The C.O. had made his twenty-first kill.

Just two days later Plt Off Edwards failed to return from a recce flight to Dieppe. The C.O. took off immediately to look for him but had to abandon the search when attacked by an FW 190. The New Zealand pilot, 'Scotty' Downer, also failed to return from his dawn recce patrol. Roger Hall came down to breakfast to learn that 'Scotty' was dead. Both had flown on numerous recces together. The surviving pilot explained to the IO how he had seen two Bf 109s emerge from cloud to sit on 'Scotty's' tail. It was one of those moments when reflexes become paralysed. Overwrought and emotional the young and comparatively inexperienced pilot apologised profusely to the C.O.

Flt Lt Andrews celebrated his twenty-first birthday by attacking a goods train near Ostend, and whilst returning, blasted a merchant ship off Zeebrugge. Andrews, who had flown a Spitfire for the film sequences in 'The First Of The Few', was reported missing soon afterwards. It happened when

156

Sqdn Ldr Jean Demozay, Order of Liberation, Croix de Guerre, DFC, and Bar, with pilots of 'B' Flight No 91 (Nigerian) squadron at Hawkinge September 1942.   (Kent Messenger)

both he and Jean Maridor were up on dawn patrol. For some time now the recces had been flown in pairs. They were near the Belgian coast when they were met by five FW 190s. In the ensuing combat two enemy machines were destroyed but Andrews was killed. Maridor, his Spitfire riddled with bullet holes just managed to limp back to Hawkinge. It was soon after this incident that he was awarded the DFC.

Another experienced fighter pilot of the squadron was to die, the nineteen-year-old Plt Off de-Moline, a Frenchman born in Lyons. Flt Lt Hall with de-Moline as his wingman, took off to look for a bomber crew who were reported somewhere between Dungeness and Le Touquet. de-Moline seemed agitated about something for he was making hand signals to Roger. Thinking his radio was most probably out of order, Roger signalled to him to close up as weather reports suggested fog later. They flew Southwards in shallow 'S' turns in a hazy visibility. They had gone beyond the half-way mark and, in a final wide sweep to port, avoided the low-lying mass of France, keeping low to the water to evade the shore flak batteries.

They eventually located the yellow dinghy and, by way of hand signals, de-Moline was despatched to meet the launch. Low on fuel Roger had to leave the area and expected to see his wingman refuelling on his arrival but he had not returned. Refuelling completed Roger, with another pilot, took off for the Dungeness area where they saw some three miles from the coast a collection of small boats, among them an RAF launch. The exhilaration at finding the

157

Pilots of No 91 (Nigerian) squadron round Annie's Tea Van, Hawkinge 1942. Left to right:—
Plt Off Demoline – Ronny Ingram – Johnny Edwards – Billy Orr – Bill Heap – Lambert alias
Copeland – Scotty Downer.   (D. Hartwell)

dinghy was now overshadowed by the obvious loss of de-Moline. It transpired
that the Frenchman had approached the launch with a petrol-starved engine.
The crew watched the Spitfire turn upside down and the pilot leave the cockpit
only to have his parachute entangled with the tailplane. The parachute never
opened.

The highly decorated Sqdn Ldr 'Moses' Demozay, DSO, DFC, and a Bar
was promoted to Wing Commander and went to Dover as Air Liaison
Officer. 'Moses', who had once shot down an enemy fighter into the streets
of Boulogne, was given a great send off. It was a party to end all parties and
one where Flt Lt Chris Le Roux celebrated a Bar to his DFC.

Demozay's successor, Sqdn Ldr Ray Harries, DFC, was already a well
known personality and was to have a final score of twenty victories, but
even Harries' popularity was eclipsed by the new Station Commander, Wing
Commander L. Strange, DSO, DFC and Bar, MC who had flown from
Hawkinge in the First World War. He had rejoined the RAF in 1940 as a
Pilot Officer at the age of forty-nine.

Whilst the orientation of Flights to serve at nearby Lympne became a
necessity because of a Group decision, ground crew, under vigorous protests
were detailed to occupy the passenger cockpit of an ancient Tiger Moth.
While some airmen may have been under the misapprehension that it was
joyriding, others realised the importance of reminding them of their skills.
However, when ashen-faced 'erks' returned with stories of low flying over
topless Land Army girls there was a rush to participate!

CHAPTER ELEVEN
Special Heroics, August 1942–January 1945

Germany was now being exposed to bombing raids never before experienced in the history of air warfare. Air supremecy, only discussed in 1942, was now becoming a reality in 1943. The American 8th Air Force, stationed in England since the previous August, blasted the Third Reich in daylight, while Bomber Command on the other hand, preferred night operations.

1943 provided more opportunities for Fighter Command squadrons to operate over enemy held territories despite the formidable encounters with Germany's latest fighters. No 91 squadron at last was given the task of flying at squadron strength at sweeps, a task previously denied them, although in January they had joined No 609 squadron in routing over twenty-eight FW 190s escorted by Bf 109s returning from a lightning raid on London. Nine enemy machines were shot down.

The special photo-reconnaissance Spitfire VI, fitted with a long-range camera, was in constant use photographing dock and harbour installations, flak defences, shipping and railways before and after bombing raids. Flt Lt Batten was an expert in this type of recce and usually returned with excellent film which was developed and then rushed to Group. Although strictly for photo-recce work, the PR Spitfire was fitted with the usual compliment of cannon and machine guns like any other fighter in the squadron. Batten could never pass-up an opportunity to blast troop barges, shipping and flak batteries. But on 9th February he remained too long in chasing a Dornier across the Channel and well into France where he ran out of petrol and was taken prisoner.

Perhaps it was that which influenced the station C.O. to organise an escape exercise two weeks later. Twenty-seven 'would-be' escapers, made up of both pilots and airmen from 91 and 277 squadrons, were dropped from a lorry in isolated areas in pairs and were told to make their own way back to the aerodrome undetected.

Under the inspired leadership of Sqdn Ldr Palmer, VC, a veteran of the First World War, over one hundred fully armed men of the RAF Regiment were defending the airfield perimeters. The first success was the C.O., Sqdn Ldr Harries, who had purloined an Army Officer's uniform from a house near Elham, and who managed to walk through the road-blocks without being challenged once! With spontaneous ingenuity and a patter likely to charm the birds out of the trees, Plt Off Hartwell and Warrant Officer Waddington, both of 277 squadron, assisted by Land Army girls, temporarily borrowed a milk float. Dressed in hastily acquired Land Army

Sergeant Pilot D. Waddington of No 277 (Air Sea Rescue) squadron Hawkinge.
(D. Waddington)

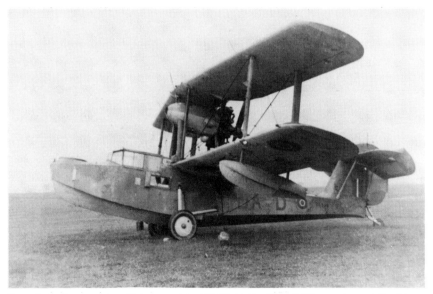

One of the Supermarine Walrus used by 'B' Flight No 277 (ASR) squadron at Hawkinge 1942–43.(C. G. Curran)

Pilots and crew scramble to their aircraft of No 277 (ASR) squadron at Hawkinge 1943.
(Imperial War Museum)

dungerees they calmly guided horse and float through barriers to deliver eggs to the Officers' Mess!

On 25th May the C.O. and three others of 91 squadron were in circuit ready to land when an order to scramble came over the R/T. Fifteen 'bandits' had been monitored on the radar screens heading for Folkestone. With undercarriages rapidly being wound up, the new MK XII Griffin engined Spitfires shot away from the airfield boundary. They met the raiders just one mile from Folkestone harbour, head-on. Taken by surprise the raiders released their bombs too early to be any danger to the town. Maridor's cannons made short work of the leading machine which spun into the sea with a terriffic full-boosted dive sending great plumes of spray into the air. Harries reached two fleeing FW 190s and shot both down. A new pilot to the squadron, Round, raced after one and eventually caught it three miles from the French coast where it blew up.

In all five enemy aircraft were credited to the squadron without loss to themselves. They became heroes that night. The Chief Constable telephoned the aerodrome thanking them for saving Folkestone from what might have been a disasterous raid. Telegrams and letters followed and, on 3rd June, a reception in honour of the squadron was held at Bobby's restaurant. A sequel to this concerns Nigeria, who bestowed twenty-four silver tankards on the unit in tribute to their gallant action.

Sergeants Fletcher, Healey and Glew, otherwise known on the airfield as the 'Three Musketeers' of the air sea rescue unit, were sent off in their faithful Walrus to rescue six men reported seen on a raft in mid-Channel. The weather was deteriorating fast when they arrived over the area. High winds and lashing seas prevented a quick sighting of the raft. Fletcher, his knuckles white with the strain of keeping the amphibian flying, brought it

Flt Lt 'Jackie' Spence, a Canadian who flew with No 277 (ASR) squadron. (D. Hartwell)

Sgt 'Sticker' Glew of No 277 (ASR) squadron, who was to lose his life flying in Malta. (D. Hartwell)

round time and again into the teeth of a gale. Considerable time elapsed before the raft was seen. Fletcher brought the Walrus down wind then turned back towards the raft and made a heavy landing that sent the craft bouncing from wave top to wave top. But he kept the Walrus heading into wind to allow the raft to drift to his port side. As it drew near Sgt Glew stretched out with the boathook but instead of making fast, one of the men grabbed it and leaped onto the amphibian. Buffeted by the high swell the raft immediately swept past. As it cleared the side of the hull a huge wave smashed over it sweeping two men overboard who were soon lost in the inky darkness. By now the Walrus was shipping water continuously. The starboard windshield had been smashed. The electrical system started to short and give off sparks and the cabin began to fill with acrid smoke. Up to his knees in water, Healey managed to haul one of the men through the after-hatch. Turning a third time, Fletcher steered towards the bobbing raft where Glew snatched and held another, but his companion was swept over the side and vanished. Although it was now getting quite dark by this time Fletcher continued to search for the lost men. Forced to give up he set course for Dover. The Walrus refused to fly. Buffeted by tremendous seas and with an overheating engine the great breakwater of Dover harbour loomed through the darkness after an interminable and extremely hazardous rescue operation. Sitting huddled together on the water laden floor of the Walrus the three drenched and almost frozen individuals turned out to be German seamen whose ship had gone down after striking a mine!

A similar experience befell Flt Lt 'Jackie' Spence, a Canadian who had just rescued Sgt Ticklepenny of No 3 squadron on 15th June. It had been impossible to take off in the rough seas and so he set course for Dover. The only difference was that the escorting fighters were battling with the dreaded FW 190s most of the way. Spence had no idea there was a fight going on until he met one of 91 squadron's pilots who had been shot down and was picked up by an RAF launch!

Destined to join No 85 Group of the 2nd Tactical Air Force, No 91 squadron moved from Hawkinge towards the end of June. They had, during their stay, been a most popular unit. Their high morale, keenness of spirit and dedicated flying had won them a fantastic record of 77 enemy aircraft destroyed, 27 probables and 78 damaged. They had gained a DSO, eleven DFCs, four Bars and five DFMs.

The airfield was not to remain long without a resident fighter unit and on 21st June No 501 squadron arrived with their Spitfire MK Vs. They were to change these for MK IXs before the end of the year, and a common sight during their stay were Spitfires returning from sorties with an assortment of continental shrubbery protruding from radiators and telegraph wire trailing from tail wheels! Combat opportunities were lessening as the Luftwaffe units kept clear of our shores. The squadron, however, was becoming adept at following in the wake of mass daylight bombing raids to photograph the damage.

It had always been accepted that Hawkinge was a difficult airfield on which to land with anything more than two engines. With a four engined bomber it was like trying to land on a pocket handkerchief! Additional field length had been provided however, which ran into a meadow on the north side of Aerodrome Road. Alerted when a stricken bomber was making a bee-line for the aerodrome, ground personnel rushed out to move fences across the road, thus extending the landing length.

This had already been accomplished when one summer's evening a seriously damaged Lancaster, with two of its engines knocked out, managed to settle on the grass after repeated attempts. Brakes squeeling the Lancaster of No 460 squadron continued on its course towards the village and failed to negotiate a turn to port into the extension meadow. Instead, it tore into a hastily vacated Nissen hut which split apart like a ruptured melon.

By mid-1943, one lived in an atmosphere heavy with speculation about the so-called second front. One plan after another took shape only to be superceded by the next. The final plan, codenamed 'Overlord', found its origin in a number of diversionary schemes one of which was called 'Starkey'. As any threat of an allied invasion by a large amphibian operation in the Pas de Calais area would almost certainly have aroused the German high command's suspicions, it was only natural to give that impression in that particular area. It was never intended to send our forces into battle but to monitor the enemy's reaction.

Air supremacy was the ultimate weapon, and to this end, squadrons of Fighter Command arrived at Hawkinge. Starkey began to take shape in early August and produced a remarkable increase in enemy air activity, especially high flying reconnaissance flights to see what was going on!

No 313 (Czech) squadron was at Hawkinge and was scrambled on the evening of 27th August to intercept FW 190s who were heading towards the aerodrome. They were actually taking off whilst the Bofors were engaging their targets.

In the first week of September 'Starkey' got underway with the ships of the Royal Navy steaming up and down the Channel in full view of the German coastal gun batteries. Overhead hundreds of American and British fighters and fighter-bombers, roared across the sea in one of the biggest shows of force yet seen. Flight Sergeant Quintin of No 165 squadron enjoyed the view from his dinghy some fifteen miles out from Hastings, despite the turbulent waves which broke over him leaving him covered in yellow dye that he had liberally sprinkled upon the water. But in a few hours the whole operation wound down. Months of preparation bringing air, sea and land forces together in one huge exercise ground to a halt.

The Czechoslovakian squadron were operating sweeps and escorted a number of Bostons, Mitchells and Marauders who were bombing railway marshalling yards at low level. They lost Sgt J. Green when he flew into high ground at Wormshill, Kent, and very nearly lost Flt Lt Rejthar who suffered an engine failure whilst taking off.

The twenty-four-hour ordeal of Plt Off Turek, No 609 squadron, goes a long way to illustrate the persistent devotion of the rescue squadron at Hawkinge. Turek had abandoned his Typhoon near the French coast late on 20th September. A Walrus was despatched immediately with two Spitfires as escort. Turek was spotted about ten miles from the mouth of the Somme estuary in an extremely rough sea. Smoke floats and a dinghy were dropped but the smoke floats failed to ignite. By this time the fuel situation was almost critical and the Walrus was ordered to return. At 18.00 hrs Sgt Moore took off in one of the ASR Spitfires to orbit Turek and relieve the original escort. Moore released four smoke floats to keep his customer in view for by then it was getting dark. Turek must have been heartened by the attempts to rescue him. Moore was relieved by a Walrus at 19.00 hrs and, despite the twilight, Turek was soon found. Sqdn Ldr Brown in the amphibian decided to deliver additional illumination. A Mae West was inflated in which were placed flares and an electric torch, and was dropped together with another dinghy. Turek watched the Walrus going round and round with no hope of alighting on the turbulent water, then it was ordered back to base. The luckless pilot settled down to wait. He was alone and was to remain so for the rest of the night.

But at first light three Spitfires of 501 squadron took off to relocate Turek, closely followed by a Walrus piloted by Plt Off Standen with Sgt Wilson and W.O. Bruckenhorst as crew. A pair of 609 squadron Typhoons joined them and, fifty-six miles out from Dungeness, the yellow dinghy was eventually sighted. Standen decided to risk it and put the Walrus down on a twelve feet swell. It hopped from one wave top to another in incredible leaps. But at last the patiently waiting Turek, shivering with cold and soaked to the skin, was hauled aboard. As Standen opened the throttle for take off he saw great plumes of water gush up in front of the Walrus, as German shells were bombarding the area. Unable to take off in the swell he steered the Walrus out of harms way and set course for Dover. At 11.00 hrs they were met by a launch who towed them onto the beach at Dungeness.

Four days later No 313 squadron lost their C.O., whilst escorting Mitchells over Northern France. They ran into a large formation of Messerschmitt 110s which successfully shot down two of the squadron Spitfires. Sqdn Ldr Fatjl, DFC, took over the unit for the remainder of its stay at Hawkinge. Fatjl had been reported missing in 1942 and had been taken prisoner. He escaped and got back to the U.K.

Nearly all the bombing raids made by aircraft of No 2 Group, were softening-up attacks on enemy installations prior to the impending invasion of France. One of the most successful raids made by Bostons was in November when the village of Audinghen, suspected of being the HQ of the German Todt organisation was, according to photographic evidence taken later, entirely obliterated.

It was whilst turning away from this attack that a Boston of No 88 squadron, piloted by Plt Off Gibson, was hit by flak. Gibson received a fractured collar bone which rendered him momentarily unconscious. Though suffering from near paralysis of the arms he guided the plunging aircraft back onto an even keel, then ordered his crew to bale out. No one moved.

Gibson found Hawkinge with the help of two Spitfires of No 501 squadron and with great difficulty set it down on the grass. A heavily damaged Mitchell of No 180 squadron was not so lucky when it ran out of fuel whilst in circuit and crashed into a wood nearby.

Since the previous month No 350 (Belgian) squadron, under the command of Sqdn Ldr Boussa, had been operating from the airfield with Spitfire Vbs. It was made up of Belgian nationals, many of whom had escaped from their own country and had distinguished themselves notably in the Dieppe raid during which they had destroyed seven enemy aircraft. At Hawkinge they flew Ramrods, Rhubarbs and bomber escorts in quite foul weather conditions.

Another unit to share facilities was the Dutch No 322 squadron who arrived on the day the Belgians left. Already in 132 Wing of the newly formed No 84 Group of the 2nd TAF, they had been formed at Hornchurch on 12th June that year and consisted mostly of Dutch nationals. Commanded by Major K. C. Kuhlmann, DFC, they operated the usual Channel patrols until they were fully operational. As a fully fledged fighter squadron in the new year they carried out Ramrods and bomber escorts and completed over 150 sorties in one month.

Five or more operational sorties a day, weather permitting, kept the gunners on their toes. The RAF Regiment manning the defences were so keen to have a go, irrespective of what nationality the aircraft belonged to, that they had subsequently to be rationed with ammunition! They felt their own contribution to the war effort was sadly lacking in intensity since the virtual disappearance of the Luftwaffe. They often complained they had nothing to fire at, except for the occasional American fighters who always seemed to approach the airfield from under the cliffs. Naturally the gunners fired first and then asked questions afterwards! But out of a particularly dark January night sky at 21.00 hrs, the Luftwaffe suddenly appeared to make up for lost time. A dispersal hut was blown to pieces, another caught alight and the area became a shambles with several airmen injured. Searchlights stabbed the sky and night-fighters claimed three enemy aircraft destroyed.

When both 501 and 322 squadrons escorted over 50 Marauders bombing targets in the St Omer vicinity, the fighter pilots could only thank their lucky stars that they were weaving around as top cover and quite unmolested. They watched the light-bombers flying into fierce flak and saw crippled aircraft turn over, some alight, some with wings torn off, to spin groundwards out of control. They counted the parachutes and watched in horror as airmen fell out of blazing fuselages without them.

It was the Dutch squadron's turn to suffer casualties. Flg Off De Neve's Spitfire dived into the ground near the airfield during a mock dog-fight with Typhoons. When the unit scrambled at 11.55 hrs on 28th January, to intercept enemy aircraft in the south east, Flg Offs Van Nagell and Walters somehow found they were over Calais amidst intensive flak. Van Nagell was last seen well in-land flying in an easterly direction. He failed to return.

When His Royal Highness Prince Bernard of the Netherlands arrived at Hawkinge to present medals to airmen of the Dutch Air Force, three medals remained in their boxes unopened.

It was generally agreed that No 501 squadron's move to Hawkinge was considered a rest period between the lull and the storm to come! In some ways they emulated the previous 'Jim Crow' unit by having a mixture of European born pilots who were now flying over their own countries. One particular story of the squadron concerns a Free Frenchman Captain Fuchs, whose speciality seemed to be shooting up eney ammunition trains, and especially the 09.45 out of Abbeville! He never explained why this particular train should have been singled out in this way. But he never allowed one to get through. Fuchs was also obsessed with a Gremlin which, he insisted, always sat on his bed. He once held up a squadron strike due to this but, nonetheless, he was a brilliant pilot and was later awarded the Croix de

This USAAF Flying Fortress B17 crash-landed at Hawkinge on 15.9.43, and very nearly toppled over the airfield boundary and on to Terlingham Manor Farm. (Crown Copyright)

Guerre, DFC, and three Bars. By the time the squadron had left Hawkinge for Friston they had notched up 341 missions of all types.

There had already been many dramatic crashes on the airfield, each held its own traumatic and peculiar characteristics, like the Mosquito of No 21 squadron which had landed crab-like on one engine, the Liberator that had belly-flopped, tearing out the underside of the fuselage, and the Marauder which actually fell apart as it careered across the dew-soaked grass to end its days as a pile of rusting metal.

But one of the most dramatic crash incidents that happened when Wing Commander Mike Crossley was station C.O. occurred one afternoon when a very lame B17, returning from a bombing raid on the Continent, suddenly loomed up over the trees at Killing Wood with every intention of landing. The wheels were locked down but the port inner engine was missing, torn from its mounting by a direct hit.

"Now as you know" Mike Crossley remembered, "Hawkinge was hardly suitable for gigantic four engined bombers even when they are in the capable hands of the pilot, let alone the navigator, as this one turned out to be. The pilot and co-pilot both having been killed during the raid."

"It was soon evident that the man in charge could not, or did not know, how to get his remaining throttles right back as the poor old B17 came sailing across the grass at about ten feet and just about thirty miles an hour above the stalling speed. When he saw he couldn't make it he slammed open the throttles, and with a ghastly sort of yawing swoop, just missed the Flying Control Office with his wing tips and then disappeared below the immediate horizon of trees."

"The tarmac was by this time dotted with running figures and as the B17 disappeared everybody stopped breathing and just listened for the crash.

167

Nothing happened except the roar of the three engines kept on and on with every ear following the general line of sound. Suddenly the darned thing appeared at the same spot of entry as the last time. It was still going too fast and too high. The Flying Control Office, rather unsportingly I thought, fired off a red Very Light at him, but the unfortunate chap was in no mood to watch a firework display. He came in just the same. Well, more or less the same thing happened, but this time slightly higher and we were able to watch this unhappy progress round the circuit. There was no question in our minds as to whether he was going to crash or not, it was simply a matter of where he would crash."

"We were not held in suspense for very long. He did his turn about a mile away and, as he straightened out, we could see that one of his propellers was windmilling. Maybe he had cut the engine in an effort to slow down, anyway it nearly had the desired effect as he was now quite near the stall. I forgot to mention that he had lost his flaps somewhere along the way, so he simply did not have a chance. He slammed the nose down and came skidding in across the field with his tail in the air, looking for all the world as if searching for something. Well the field soon ran out and he charged through a fence, hit a bank, and came to rest straddled across Gibraltar Lane. The tail section broke away and deposited the tail gunner on the further side of the road where I found him forlornly sitting when I arrived on the scene moments later."

"The last I saw of Master Sergeant Katz, I shall never forget his name, he was strolling off down the road, pursued by the Medical Officer in the ambulance, repeating over and over again, "Show me the bastard who will make me fly again . . . show me the b . . .""

"The heroic navigator survived, as did Katz, but the rest of the crew were gonners. Whether from the sortie or the crash I cannot remember."

Such accidents have their lighter sides in war as in peace, and another very similar incident occurred on 1st May 1944. The American 92nd Bomber Group had raided the towns of Le Gistmont and Rheims, and a B17, named 'Fort Sack' after the American cartoon character, assigned to the 325th Bomber squadron, had two of its four engines knocked out. It was an air sea rescue Spitfire which found the crippled Flying Fortress, trailing smoke about half way across the Channel. Fortress and Spitfire arrived at Hawkinge when airmen were thinking of their NAAFI break. A dozen or so cycling airmen, bunched together and fooling around, were actually on the perimeter track when from out of nowhere, or so it seemed, there suddenly appeared 'Fort Sack' bearing down on them at great speed. It just cleared the boundary fence and flopped down on the grass. It bounced with such force that one of the oleo legs collapsed. By this time the careering machine had covered quite half of the airfield and was getting perilously near the village. Fortunately a wing dug into the ground which slewed the aircraft round into the airfield extension. The perplexed airmen leaped as one from

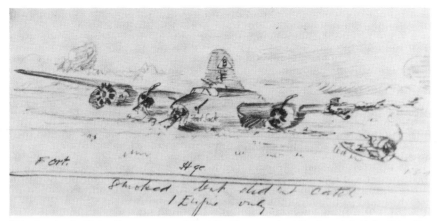

This sketch of a Flying Fortress, named 'Fort Sack' was made at the time, 1.5.44, by Brian C. Sherren. 'Fort Sack' — No 42 — 30849, operated from Podington and was part of 325th Bomber squadron of 92nd Bomber Group USAAF. It had just returned from a raid on Gristmont and Reims.

their cycles, turned them round and fled the way they had come. 'Fort Sack' came to rest in a huge cloud of dust with one wing shielding an absolutely terrified RAF Regiment gun crew.

On 23rd May Hawkinge became host to a most unusual type of aircraft when twemty-four Grumman Avengers arrived from the Royal Navy Air Station at Eglington. These torpedo-bombers belonged to Nos 854 and 855 squadrons of the Fleet Air Arm, and both units became operational by the end of that month. Carrying four depth charges as a standard load they undertook day convoy protection patrols in the Pas de Calais and lost only one Avenger on 'D'-Day plus one. From the 11th to 19th June, anti-submarine patrols (ASP) were flown to the west of the Neptune Overlord convoy routes between the Isle of Wight and Cherbourg. These were, however, in addition to the ASPs flown between North Foreland and Beachy Head. An attack was delivered on a submerging U-boat on the 12th, but as there were no signs of wreckage or oil on the water it was not claimed.

From the beginning of July they commenced night 'Rover' patrols against enemy shipping off the French, Belgian and Dutch coasts. Two 500lb and two 250lb bombs were carried with flares for target illumination and they made sixty individual attacks on small ships. However, results were difficult to observe as targets were mostly small, highly manoeuvrable craft and, although several surface vessels were assumed to have suffered damage, it was not until the 28th that No 855 squadron was rewarded by the sinking of an artillery ferry barge. The same squadron lost two Avengers during shipping attacks and lost another when it failed to clear the airfield perimeter on take off. Watching ground crews saw it tear through a fence and expected the bombs to explode.

The TBF–1 Grumman Avenger MKII, equipped both Fleet Air Arm squadrons Nos 845 and 855 when operating their Channel sweeps prior to 'Overlord'.   (Imperial War Museum)

From early 1944 all the efforts of the American and British air forces were concentrated on the preparation of 'Operation Overlord', the 'D'-Day landings. The task of co-ordinating the operations of Bomber Command and the USAAF Strategic Air Forces in Europe was colossal, but it provided round the clock bombing of vital factories in Germany. Additionally, attacks were made on the Luftwaffe to destroy the forward airfields and aircraft wherever they were found. These bombing formations required heavy fighter escorts both on the outgoing and incoming journeys, especially the American daylight raids whose losses were considerably greater than those of the British. Even so, the Luftwaffe put up tenacious resistance to these massive bombing raids which were particularly successful in March 1944, when only the American Mustang fighter was capable of escorting the formations to the very heart of Germany. The Spitfire squadrons at that time had to leave the formations at the Dutch coast returning to our own airfields for refuelling and then flying out to meet the returning bombers.

With the Normandy landing drawing near, vast areas of wooded valleys and tree-lined fields around the aerodrome held concentrations of lorries, jeeps, personnel carriers and tanks. Daubed with the allied invasion insignia, this build-up revealed a massive military target for the occasional German reconaissance aircraft. It was impossible to conceal this mighty invasion armada, for air, land and sea exercises were in operation along our coasts. Hawkinge and the surrounding areas played host to thousands of troops of all nationalities. Roads leading to the airfield had long since been blocked. Strict security was enforced by over twelve RAF Regiment squadrons.

During the first week of June all aircraft of the ADGB and 2nd TAF received black and white invasion stripes, even the amphibians. Early on 5th all station personnel were confined to camp and in the late evening all the pilots were briefed regrding the Second Front.

In the twilight of the 6th, hundreds of fighters broke the morning stillness and took off to take up their positions for the biggest invasion in history of warfare. Squadrons designated the task of creating a false warning in the Pas de Calais used Hawkinge. An additional Flying Control had been constructed of wood which stood on high ground to the west, in which personnel tried to cope with increased air traffic to the tune of over 9,000 aircraft.

The Air Sea Rescue 'B' Flight's aircraft had more than doubled with some twenty ASR Spitfires and five Walrus. Over twenty-two separate sorties had been made in just one day by the Flight and Flt Lt Mackertitch was later awarded the DFC for rescuing no fewer than 74 pilots and aircrew. Wing Commander Grace, No 277's C.O., came down to assist with the increasing demands being made on the rescue unit. Stray barrage balloons were floating around on both sides of the Channel and were becoming a menace to flying, but in the sea they were often mistaken for dinghies. The only way to deal with those semi-floating balloons was to sink them by cannon fire.

Exactly seven days after the Normandy invasion, Hitler unleashed one of the most deadly weapons yet seen. This was the V1, the pilotless rocket-propelled robot with a one ton explosive warhead. The British had known of its existence for some time and had been bombing the launching sites as early as December 1943. These sites were difficult to locate and each time we bombed them, more sites were selected and quickly became operational. The 'Doodle-bug' or 'Buzz-bomb', was something of an unknown quantity in the initial stages of its use. Its speed of about 400 mph was not at first appreciated but fortunately it was pre-set to run in a straight line at between 1,000 and 4,000 feet — a nice steady target for the guns. Operated by an auto-pilot mechanism, when the prearranged target had been reached the engine would shut off, the elevators were depressed and the robot dived to the ground. The name 'Diver' was the official RAF term and 'Diver patrols' became commonplace in the south east. Considerably smaller than the conventional fighter aircraft the V1 was thus harder to hit. Fighters approached them with extreme caution as the warhead explosion would often engulf the attacking machine causing it to crash.

By July the incredible number of 4,000 flying bombs had been launched against England, 900 of which were destroyed by our fighters. The coastal guns were later given free licence to open fire on sight and it became quite hazardous for our pilots who often ignored the AA batteries and flew through the barrage. Eventually mobile rocket-launchers were introduced and certain areas were put out of bounds to fighters.

The Canadian No 402 squadron arrived at Hawkinge especially to combat the V1 menace on 9th August, and their first success was on the 16th when they shot down three. One came down near the Flying Control Office and

Sqdn Ldr Mike Donnet, C.O. of No 350 (Belgian) squadron, with Flt Sgt Gebreucq of 'B' Flight. As Wg Cdre 'Flying', Mike Donnet later led the Hawkinge Wing.
(Lt General Aviateur Baron M. Donnet, CVO, DFC)

two operators were slightly injured by blast. Another careered onto the ground near a Bofors site. Both No 402 and No 350 squadrons managed to have over twenty Spitfires on standing patrols throughout the daylight hours, but when operating offensive sweeps over France, they found them uneventful!

Before 402 squadron left for the forward airstrip at Diest, northern France, a number of robots had been destroyed by manoeuvring a Spitfire's wing under that of the missile. With a sharp banking movement they tipped the 'Doodle-bug' into a dive.

The Belgian squadron, under the command of Sqdn Ldr M. G. L. Donnet, DFC, completed their second tour at Hawkinge and left for nearby Lympne at the end of September, to make room for No 132 squadron whose C.O. was the distinguished Malta veteran Sqdn Ldr K. L. Charney, DFC and Bar. But the Canadian drawl was again heard at the airfield when No 441 squadron arrived from their forward airstrip at Deurne, northern France. The wreckage of two crashed Lancasters seemed an ill omen for when escorting a Lancaster raid over Duisberg a week later, the Canadians watched helplessly while four of them blew up over the target area and another three went down in flames. On another raid over Germany they lost Flg Off McDonald and Plt Off Brocau who were last seen descending through cloud just south of Brussels. For these bomber escorts the Spitfires were fitted with 90-gallon drop-tanks which enabled the squadron to penetrate deeper into Europe. Ground crews swore when, having fitted the drop-tanks, were often told the squadron would not be required to escort

This drawing of a crashed Liberator at Hawkinge was made at the time on 1.3.44, by Brian C. Sherren, an artist serving with the Royal Engineers.

bombers, but instead, would be required to operate 'Diver Patrols'. 'Drop-tanks were taken off. But when Group had changed their mind yet again, the drop-tanks were refitted. It was most probably due to this confusion that a Spitfire's wing exploded on start-up and burned out to a cinder. In December the Canadians left for Scotland for a rest period and they were replaced by No 611 squadron and an Australian squadron, No 451. The latter unit was equipped with the Spitfire XVI and carried eight rockets under the wings. Primarily a ground attack fighter the 'sixteens' were used extensively in this role for long range sweeps shooting up retreating German military columns and supply routes. Both squadrons flew as the Hawkinge Wing, under Wing Commander Donnet, and on 14th January 1945 had to abandon their Ramrod because of deteriorating weather conditions on the Continent. Returning in thick fog after being in the air for 90 minutes, Flt Lt Wallis of 451 squadron was killed when his tail section was cut off by another Spitfire over Ostende. Plt Off Newbury crash-landed in the same area but he was found by an AA battery, alive but shaken.

January 1945 was cold and damp and much of the airfield became pitted with deep rutted tracks making manoeuvring of aircraft risky. By February No 277 (ASR) squadron officially disbanded, but it was arranged they should continue with two Walrus on strength until No 278 (ASR) squadron took over responsibilities. The Australians packed their bags and left for Manston, and Sqdn Ldr D. H. Seaton of 611 squadron was highly delighted to learn his unit was to receive the North American Mustang IV fighter. Only four of the new fighters arrived at Hawking before they moved to Hunsden in March.

When our Airborne Forces were crossing the Rhine, Hawkinge was used as a turning point in their navigation and for that reason a flashing beacon, giving the letters 'AI', was set up there.

The airmen's NAAFI at RAF Hawkinge is still standing although extensive housing developments surround it.

One of two Hawkinge barrack blocks built in the 1930s and although now converted into flats, they still retain their original outward appearance.

CHAPTER TWELVE

The Declining Legend, February 1945–December 1961

A succession of ENSA shows were appearing at the Gymnasium every week. They contrasted with the stark wintry setting of the snow-flecked aerodrome. Variety performances included The Squadronaires Band, Ralph Reader's Gang Shows, 'Stinker' Murdoch and Kenneth Horne, Guy Fielding and Joan Winters. With the Sky Rockets Dance Band were Claude Damper, Billy Carlisle and Dorothy Summers.

The war was now drawing to a close and the aerodrome was having its last fling. One of the last sorties of the war took place from Hawkinge when Nos 441 and 124 squadrons escorted over 400 Lancasters and Halifaxes of No 6 Group Bomber Command on Ramrod 1555 to Wangaroo Island. In May the Spitfires of 451 and 453 squadrons returned from Lympne and on 8th, Wing Commander 'Mike' Crossley made an evening broadcast from the BBC, addressing the King on behalf of the Royal Air Force. The following day a ceremonial colour-hoisting parade was held at 11.00 hrs, taken by Crossley. There was a dance organised in the evening and at midnight, an effigy of Adolf Hitler was burned on a huge bonfire.

May had a strange air about it. After the rush and tumble of so many visiting squadrons who stayed for only short periods, the sudden inactivity brought a kind of uncertainty and a substantial part of the normal working day was spent on a frenzied clean-up campaign. Surrender of the German armed forces on 8th May gave strength and purpose to airmen in their off-duty hours. The stillness of many a night was broken periodically by returning revellers from Folkestone. The collapse of the Third Reich produced a varied concoction of school boy antics. An Austin Ruby saloon car was retrieved from a hedge near Paddlesworth. A Hillman service van was seen hurtling round the perimeter track with at least thirty people hanging on for grim death. WAAFs on the station, now totalling near 300, began to check their kit when various articles of female attire were observed flying from the most exposed places. The VE Day celebrations went on for some time. No one seemed to mind what happened for the next day or so.

Mike Crossley remembered, "Discipline went a bit haywire, especially with the Aussies around! Nobody minded very much, but I had a Hell of a time to dissuade them from uprooting all the ornamental trees and shrubs around the Mess, setting fire to the nearest petrol bowser and remaining hangar! Fortunately they were all too plastered to implement their more bizarre schemes. But when I found the entire duty fire-picket paralysed as well, I decided it was time I went to bed. The fact that it took me quite ten minutes to find the Mess, which was all of a hundred yards away, was beside the point!"

Originally a sports pavilion, the sorry-looking building which once housed flares and dinghies for air sea rescue has now been demolished.

The little mortuary at Hawkinge still stands, its future uncertain.

Gradually life became normal and activity of a different sort induced a greater sense of responsibility among airmen when returning Prisoners-of-War were brought over from the Continent. The Dutch Royal Family were escorted back to Holland from Hawkinge and King Peter of Yugoslavia also returned to his country.

Inevitably, with the collapse of Japan on August 14th, more celebrations broke out but the station personnel realised that peace was finally at hand and demobilisation just around the corner. But before demob began to function with anything like the well-oiled machine it later became, the Air Ministry decided to make Hawkinge the new location for No 3 Armament Practice School. Wing Commander H. C. Kennard, DFC, received the first two squadrons to take part in peace-time during September.

Martinet and Vengence aircraft had been flown in and parked rather haphazardly near the one and only hangar, ready to be modified for drogue towing. Six airmen were employed on this so that air to ground firing could be carried out at Leysdown and air to air firing at Herne Bay and Birchington. The modified aircraft were taxied back and forth from workshops and dispersals by the fitters and mechanics of No 576 squadron, who it seemed, were exempt from the mandatory discipline of any form of NCO. They were to enjoy complete freedom from petty rules and instructions and found unforeseen pleasure in guiding those fat bellied brutes round the tarmac on any pretext.

Eventually, as all good things must come to an end, the APS was moved to the North of England and the out of work airmen were returned to their original unit at Hornchurch. Communication had, however, fouled-up somewhere for it was discovered that no one knew of their correct posting. In all seven trips back and forth to Hawkinge took place in as many weeks. Their final reception at the aerodrome was one of complete disbelief, for this little band of nomads realised, with a deal of apprehension, that they were all alone. The aerodrome was completely deserted. Aircraft and personnel had disappeared! It was now under care and maintenance, and for the next eleven months the aerodrome was manned only by civilians.

The words 'Care and Maintenance' were like a sentence of death. No more would squadrons arrive to be cared for, their aircraft fussed over, young pilots revered and respected. No more would the mess corridors echo with the boisterous babbling of youthful fighter pilots. Gone were the days of scrambles, nervous tension and soiled cockpits. Gone also the cheerful competition of 'kills', the sadness of lost friends and the binges at the local.

Memories lurk in every corner, each building holds its own. History was made here, at the dispersals, in the Flying Control Room, out on the perimeter track and in the little mortuary. The decaying buildings stand to this day like vast memorials.

It was Sqdn Ldr J. Littler who wrote in the station diary, "RAF Hawkinge, which has, since the outbreak of hostilities, played a very important role in the

Successful WAAF candidates on their march past after completing their training course at Hawkinge in 1949. (Group Captain D. M. W. Williams, WRAF)

A narrow escape for a young ATC cadet under instruction who landed on the Hawkinge village hairdresser's shop in 1956. (E. Haddow)

Once proudly displayed at Hawkinge as the gate guardian, this Spitfire Mk IX is seen here being taken away in 1961. It was moved under protest as Folkestone Council had tried to retain the aircraft for permanent display on the town's Leas. It did, however, return to Hawkinge in the summer of 1968, for a brief period, during the filming of Saltzman's epic Battle of Britain.

(E. Kettle)

defence of Great Britain and the Empire, is now closed down to care and maintenance. At no period throughout the six years of war has this station been declared non-operational, and it can only be hoped that the Air Council, in their wisdom, will find it possible to use once more an RAF station that has achieved immortal fame, and earned the gratitude of mankind in general."

But in July 1947 the arrival of the WAAF Technical Training Unit, under the command of Group Officer N. Dinnie, brought life back to the old aerodrome. Courses were run in drill and administration for other ranks and, in addition, refresher courses for WAAF officers. Those who passed out successfully from Hawkinge found themselves posted to Recruit Training Centres in various parts of the British Isles.

The immortal Spitfire appeared on static display at the aerodrome, near the guardroom entrance, and remained as a symbol of the aerodrome's former glory.

In December 1955, the Home Gliding School was set up to train the ATC cadets. The thrills of gliding were quite tame compared with powered flight, and when the flimsy canvas structures, designed to protect the aerofoils,

Her Royal Highness, Queen Elizabeth the Queen Mother, visits the station and is shown here being introduced to Dame Henrietta Barnett.

blew down in a gale, unforeseen problems arose with airmen who were posted in to repair the damage. Dressed in a mixture of service and civilian attire, the 'erks' looked like mountain bandits from outer Mongolia. Apart from making themselves very unpopular with WAAF instructors, who were busy trying to impress their charges in various forms of 'savoir faire', they held nightly sing-songs in the NAAFI round a soaking piano and provided trainees with a congenial, if somewhat bawdy, insight into service life!

The WRAF OCTU courses previously of three months duration were extended to six months with the February 1961 intake. The young ladies were drawn from a real cross-section of society, many had fathers of Air Commodore or Group Captain rank, some were Army Officers' daughters and others orphan girls from broken homes. After kitting out with tailored uniforms there was usually a mad scramble for cuff-links, an item few had thought they would need in their wardrobes!

The girls were introduced to square-bashing, camping under canvas, map reading and route marches, the latter under the auspicies of an RAF Regiment Flight Lieutenant and a sergeant. The patience of these two male instructors coping with a gaggle of giggling teenagers, had to be seen to be believed. Most of the girls wore their pyjama trousers under their ordinary trousers for the route marches to stop the rough material from chafing their

Dame Henrietta Barnett saying good-bye to the Officers' Mess staff prior to the station close-down.

legs. It was a common sight therefore, to come across a file of officer-cadets, trudging along the byways with pyjamas flapping about like clandestine banners, with the incoherent raving of their instructors falling about their ears with inexpressible futility. Towards the end of their six months each cadet sat through hundreds of feet of film on first-aid and several girls keeled over when a particular realistically simulated colour film of an air crash came on the screen. But at the end of it all the successful candidates were commissioned into the Womens Royal Air Force.

It was at dusk on Friday 8th December 1961 that the Royal Air Force Station Hawkinge disappeared, with dignity and ceremony, from public view and entered a world of obscurity. A cold wind blew across the airfield as RAF and WRAF personnel marched and paraded with the Central Band. Prayers and blessings took place in front of No 1 hangar, the only survivor from the ravages of war. The Last Post was sounded as the RAF Ensign slowly descended for the last time in over forty years. Finally, in the presence of that most senior and distinguished of a long line of station commanders, Marshal of the Royal Air Force, Sir William Dickson, GCB, KBE, DSO, AFC, the march past took place.

Speeches over, eminent guests were whisked away into the darkness. It had been a nostalgic moment for most. All present on this sad occasion were proud to have paid tribute to this once famous aerodrome.

EPILOGUE

Seven years later on a quiet Sunday afternoon in mid-June 1968, film director Harry Saltzman arrived with his entourage of cameramen, actors, scene shifters and one hundred and one others required to shoot the film sequences. He transformed the aerodrome back to its former wartime colour and sounds, to produce scenes for that epic film 'The Battle of Britain'.

For two weeks the old airfield and the surrounding countryside were subjected to the sounds and sights of wartime Britain, and it is difficult to describe the emotions of those present when surviving fighters from that era arrived. There were many present who had first-hand knowledge and who had experienced the battles fought in the skies over South East England.

Wooden huts, dispersals and mock hangars were erected on the exact locations of the originals. Bomb craters appeared in the field to simulate the 1940 air attacks. Static aircraft, mostly Spitfires of various kinds and no longer air-worthy, stood proudly on the grass verges as if given a new lease of life.

Film sequences were shot in a mixture of bright sunlight and occasional rain showers. But, in no time at all, it was all over. In the third week, the aerodrome was once again deserted and resumed its placid existence where cattle grazed over the green expanse which had, for over fifty years, been a legend in the defence of this country.

APPENDICES

1. STATION COMMANDERS
2. INTER-WAR SQUADRON COMMANDERS
3. SQUADRONS — AIRCRAFT — UNITS — COMMANDERS

LIST OF STATION COMMANDERS

1917	Major McRae.
4.11.35	Sqdn Ldr W. F. Dickson, DSO, OBE, AFC.
17.2.36	Sqdn Ldr A. C. Bayley.
22.9.37	Wing Commander R. H. George, MC.
7.3.39	Wing Commander L. Darvall, M.C.
27.10.39	Sqdn Ldr L. S. Weedon.
30.11.39	Sqdn Ldr A. Ferris.
1.5.40	Wing Commander W. L. Payne.
10.7.40	Sqdn Ldr H. B. Hurley.
16.8.40	Wing Commander E. E. Arnold, AFC.
2.4.41	Wing Commander W. M. Fry, MC.
19.1.42	Wing Commander W. L. Bateman.
30.4.42	Wing Commander R. W. Bundey, DFC.
25.9.42	Wing Commander D. G. Jones, DSO, DFC.
2.11.42	Wing Commander W. A. Richardson.
20.12.42	Wing Commander L. L. A. Strange, DSO, DFC, MC.
11.2.43	Wing Commander F. F. Barrett.
9.1.44	Wing Commander D. J. Scott, DSO, DSC.
1.3.44	Wing Commander R. F. Watts.
1.1.45	Wing Commander M. N. Crossley, DSO, DFC.
3.9.45	Wing Commander H. C. Kennard, DFC.
1.6.47	Group Officer N. Dinnie (WAAF).
15.2.50	Group Officer A. Stephens, MBE (WAAF).
3.11.52	Group Officer M. H. Barnett, OBE (WRAF).
29.5.56	Group Officer J. L. A. Conan-Doyle, OBE (WRAF).
20.4.59	Group Officer F. B. Hill, OBE (WRAF).
13.5.60	Wing Officer E. M. Benson (WRAF).

LIST OF PRE-WAR SQUADRON COMMANDERS

No 25 Squadron

1.7.20	Sqdn Ldr Sir N. R. A. D. Leslie.
16.2.23	Sqdn Ldr A. H. Peck.
12.9.26	Sqdn Ldr E. D. Atkinson.
11.4.27	Sqdn Ldr W. H. Park.
1.1.29	Sqdn Ldr L. G. S. Payne.
19.2.30	Sqdn Ldr R. S. Aitken.
3.10.30	Sqdn Ldr H. M. Probyn.
11.2.32	Sqdn Ldr W. E. G. Bryant.
28.2.33	Sqdn Ldr A. L. Paxton.
21.1.35	Sqdn Ldr W. F. Dixon.
21.2.36	Sqdn Ldr H. H. Down.
10.9.37	Sqdn Ldr D. M. Fleming.
30.1.39	Sqdn Ldr J. R. Hallings-Pott.

No 56 Squadron

1.11.22	Sqdn Ldr I. T. Lloyd.

No 17 Squadron

1.4.24	Sqdn Ldr J. Leacroft.

No 2 (AC) Squadron

1935	Sqdn Ldr N. L. Desoer.
1938	Sqdn Ldr W. A. Opie.
1939	Sqdn Ldr A. J. W. Geddes.

SQUADRONS, UNITS AND COMMANDERS CONNECTED WITH RAF HAWKINGE

DATE	SQUADRON OR UNIT	AIRCRAFT TYPES	COMMANDER
1915–1918	No 12 Aeroplane Despatch Section	Various	Major McRae
1919–	No 120 Squadron (Air Mail)	DH9 DH10	
1920–1939	No 25 (F) Squadron	Avro 504 Snipe 7F1 Snipe 7F1 Grebe Grebe Siskin IIIa Siskin IIIa Siskin IIIa Fury I Fury I Fury II Fury II Demon Gladiator Blenheim 1F	Sqdn Ldr Sir N. R. A. Leslie Sqdn Ldr A. H. Peck Sqdn Ldr E. D. Atkinson Sqdn Ldr W. H. Park Sqdn Ldr L. G. S. Payne Sqdn Ldr R. S. Aitken Sqdn Ldr H. M. Probyn Sqdn Ldr W. E. G. Bryant Sqdn Ldr A. L. Paxton Sqdn Ldr W. F. Dickson Sqdn Ldr H. H. Down Sqdn Ldr D. M. Fleming Sqdn Ldr J. R. Hallings-Pott
1922–1923	No 56 (F) Squadron	Snipe 7F1	Sqdn Ldr I. T. Lloyd

DATE	SQUADRON OR UNIT	AIRCRAFT TYPE	COMMANDER
1924–1926	No 17 (F) Squadron	Snipe 7F1 Woodcock	Sqdn Ldr J. Leacroft
1926–1937	Wessex Area Storage	Various	
1935–1940	No 2 (Army Co-operation) Squadron	Audax Hector Lysander Avro 621 Avro 681	Sqdn Ldr N. L. Desoer Sqdn Ldr W. A. Opie Sqdn Ldr A. J. W. Geddes
1930s	No 33 (B) Squadron	Hart	Annual Summer Camp
1940–1944	No 501 (County of Gloucester) Squadron	Hurricane Spitfire V	Sqdn Ldr H. A. V. Hogan Sqdn Ldr B. Barthold Sqdn Ldr M. G. Barnett
1930s	No 502 (County of Ulster) Squadron	Virginia	Annual Summer Camp
1930s	No 503 (County of Lincoln) Squadron	Hart Hind	Annual Summer Camp
1930s	No 504 (County of Nottingham) Squadron	Wallace Horsley Hind	Annual Summer Camp
1945		Spitfire IX	Sqdn Ldr M. Kellett

Squadron	Aircraft	Notes	Year
No 600 (City of London) Squadron	Hart / Demon	Annual Summer Camp	1930s
No 601 (County of London) Squadron	Hart / Demon	Annual Summer Camp	1930s
	Hurricane	Sqdn Ldr L. Guinness	1940
No 602 (City of Glasgow) Squadron	Wapiti / Hinds	Annual Summer Camp	1930s
No 603 (City of Edinburgh) Squadron	Hart / Gladiator	Annual Summer Camp	1930s
No 604 (County of Middlesex) Squadron	Demon	Annual Summer Camp	1930s
No 605 (County of Warwick) Squadron	Hurricane	Sqdn Ldr Perry	1940
No 610 (County of Chester) Squadron	Hart / Spitfire	Annual Summer Camp / Sqdn Ldr A. T. Smith / Sqdn Ldr J. Ellis	1930s / 1940
No 612 (County of Aberdeen) Squadron	Hectors	Annual Summer Camp	1930s
No 613 (City of Manchester) Squadron	Hind	Annual Summer Camp	1930s
No 611 (West Lancashire) Squadron	Spitfire IX	Sqdn Ldr McGregor	1944
No 614 (County of Glamorgan) Squadron	Hector	Annual Summer Camp	1930s

DATE	SQUADRON OR UNIT	AIRCRAFT TYPE	COMMANDER
1940	No 615 (County of Surrey) Squadron	Hurricane	Sqdn Ldr J. R. Kayll
1942	No 616 (South Yorkshire) Squadron	Spitfire VI	Sqdn Ldr H. L. I. Brown
1939–1940	No 3 Squadron	Hurricane	Sqdn Ldr P. Gifford
1940–	No 1 Pilotless Aircraft Unit	Queen Bee Tiger Moth	
1940	Operation 'Dynamo' Back Component HQ		
1940	No 245 Squadron	Hurricane	Sqdn Ldr E. W. Whiteley
1940	No 1 Squadron	Hurricane	Sqdn Ldr D. A. Pemberton
1945		Spitfire F21	Sqdn Ldr R. S. Nash
1940–1942–1943	No 41 Squadron	Spitfire I	Sqdn Ldr C. J. Fee Sqdn Ldr H. R. L. Hood
1945		Spitfire XIV	Sqdn Ldr T. F. Neil Sqdn Ldr J. B. Shepherd
1940	No 32 Squadron	Hurricane	Sqdn Ldr J. Worrall
1940	No 64 Squadron	Spitfire	Sqdn Ldr Henstock
1940	No 72 Squadron	Spitfire	Sqdn Ldr A. R. Collins

1940	No 79 Squadron	Hurricane	Sqdn Ldr J. H. Hayworth
1940	No 141 Squadron	Defiant	Sqdn Ldr W. Richardson
1940	No 111 Squadron	Hurricane	Sqdn Ldr J. Thompson
1940	No 421 Flight	Spitfire IIa	Sqdn Ldr C. P. Green
1941–1942–1943	No 91 (Nigerian) Squadron	Spitfire IIa Spitfire V Spitfire IX Spitfire XII	Sqdn Ldr C. P. Green Sqdn Ldr R. W. Oxspring Sqdn Ldr Demozay (FF) Sqdn Ldr R. H. Harries
1941–1942–1943 1944–1945	No 277 (Air Sea Rescue) Squadron	Lysander Walrus Spitfire ASR Defiant Sea Otter	Flt Lt Young Sqdn Ldr Grice
1942	No 65 Squadron	Spitfire Vb	Sqdn Ldr A. C. Bartley
1942	No 416 Squadron	Spitfire Vb	Sqdn Ldr L. V. Chadburn
1943	No 313 (Czechoslovakian) Squadron	Spitfire Vb	Sqdn Ldr J. Himr Sqdn Ldr F. Fatjl

DATE	SQUADRON OR UNIT	AIRCRAFT TYPE	COMMANDER
1943–1944	No 350 (Belgian) Squadron	Spitfire Vb Spitfire XIV	Sqdn Ldr A. L. T. J.Boussa Sqdn Ldr M. G. L. Donnet
1943–1944	No 322 (Dutch) Squadron	Spitfire Vb Spitfire XIV	Sqdn Ldr K. C. Kuhlmann
1944	No 402 (Canadian) Squadron	Spitfire XIV	Sqdn Ldr W. G. Dodd
1944–1945	No 441 (Canadian) Squadron	Spitfire IX Mustang III	Sqdn Ldr R. H. Walker
1944–1945	No 451 (Australian) Squadron	Spitfire IX Spitfire XVI	Sqdn Ldr G. W. Small
1944	No 132 Squadron	Spitfire IX	Sqdn Ldr K. L. Charney
1945	No 124 Squadron	Spitfire IX	Sqdn Ldr G. W. Scott
1945	No 453 (Australian) Squadron	Spitfire LFXVI	Sqdn Ldr E. A. R. Essau
1945	No 122 Squadron	Spitfire IX	Sqdn Ldr Lovell
1944	No 854 Fleet Air Arm Squadron	Avenger	Lt Comd W. J. Mainprice, RN